HOW TO ANALYZE PEOPLE

A mastery to Learn how to Read People, Analyze Body Language & Personality Types, Deception Empathic, NPL, Behavioral Human, Defend Yourself from Mind Control.

BY BRANDON TRAVIS

1

Introduction

One would be surprised at how much easier it becomes to manipulate people when you know how to read their nonverbal communication. If information is king in the game of manipulation, then reading people is the queen as it allows you to almost see their thoughts.

Body language:

Proximity-Proximity is one of the easiest ways to see how people feel about you or other people. Depending on the person's culture, you can often see how comfortable or intimate someone is around you or other people by looking at how close they stand or sit to them. The less comfortable they are, the greater the distance they're likely to put between themselves and others.

Posture:

Head posture- the way someone moves or holds their heads can tell you a lot about where they are in their own head. Watching where they point their chin can tell you if they are confident, the chin will be up; aggressive, the chin will be up and pointed forward; or insecure or sad, the chin will probably facing down.

Open posture- a good way of seeing if someone is warming up to you or someone else is to see if their body is open and relaxed, usually exposing their chest. This is most common in men. Women will sometimes lean in and point their body towards you to show interest in you or what you're saying.

Closed posture- this is a good way of telling if someone is uninterested in or unsure of a certain place or interaction. They will usually hunch more as if preparing to fall asleep or duck if the situation calls for it.

Arms and legs:

Hand positions- where people place their hands says a lot about what they want. While people are familiar with how to read touching of other parties, they seldom realize how the movements and positions of the hands can be a form of sub-communication as well.

Unconscious pointing- some people, depending on how gestures are viewed in their culture, are likely to point their hands or fingers in the direction they may want to go without realizing it.

Concealed hands- someone trying to hide their hands by folding them, putting them in their pockets or behind their backs can often show defensiveness or deceptiveness. They are instinctively trying to hide a part of themselves.

Holding the head up- people using one hand to hold their head up is normally a sign that they are paying attention the best they can. Holding their heads up with both hands is more likely to mean they are bored and ready to leave or fall asleep.

Creating barrier- people keeping their arms or some object they're holding in front of them can often mean they are using it as a barrier between themselves and whoever they're interacting with. This can usually show disinterest, boredom or uncertainty.

Crossing arms- this is not always to be seen as a sign of disinterest or even negative emotion. In a lot of cases, confident people will cross their arms when they are feeling comfortable or in charge. So this one must be read with the context in mind.

Hands on hips- this is one of those positions that require context to understand. While this gesture can often be seen as a show of anger, it can also show confidence, depending on where the person is from and their culture.

Feet pointing- the feet can often give some people's intentions away as they are the easiest things to forget during an interaction since they are the farthest body part from the brain. Peoples' feet are most likely to point where the person actually wants to be.

Legs crossed- depending on where the person grew up, the way they cross their legs can usually tell you how comfortable they are depending on whether their legs cross and lean towards or away from the person they are interacting with.

Facial expressions

Happiness- this will usually come in the form of a smile where the lips pull back and up. Their cheeks will usually lift and crow's feet will form around their eyes. Only around one in ten people can fake the crow's feet around the eyes.

Sadness- the inner corners of the eyebrows will usually draw together and up while the mouth pouts and lips turn down at the corners. The jaw will usually come forward. This is considered one of the most difficult faces to fake.

Surprise- the eyebrows will rise, stretching the skin beneath them while wrinkling the skin above them. The jaw will usually loosen or drop while the eyes will open up wider, making the whites of the eyes more visible.

Fear- similar to when surprised, the eyebrows will rise, but this time in a straight line rather than a curved one and the wrinkles will be closer to the center of than across the forehead. The upper whites of the eyes usually show while the jaw loosens to scream (flight) or breathe (fight).

Anger- the lower jaw comes forward and the eyebrows are drawn together and down forming vertical wrinkles between the eyebrows. The lips will tighten or form a square depending on what the person.

Disgust- the upper lip will usually be raised, along with the lower lip. The nose will also wrinkle and the cheeks will rise up. Lines will form below the lower eyelid. This is the face most people make when smelling something bad.

Contempt-this is the easiest one to spot as one side of the mouth will rise, creating a sort of smirk. The rest of the face will often remain relaxed.

So, it was seen that it is very simple to manipulate and control people through simple means including love flooding, sulking, restricting choices, reverse psychology, and semantic (using the power of words) psychology to coerce others to do things they believed they would never do.

Chapter 1 - The Importance Of Analyzing People

Your capacity to analyses people might determine whether you will succeed or fail. Human beings are social animals. We almost always need the input of other human beings in order to achieve our important life goals. But what happens if we take on people that are unfit for their roles? We suffer defeat. Thus, it is of utmost importance to be able to analyze people. The following are some of the benefits of analyzing people.

It helps you know your allies

Whether you like it or not, the entire world will not take a liking to you. Some people will be for you, and other people will be against you. In order to maximize your chances of success, you must work with people who like you, while ignoring those who dislike you. Your capability to analyze people will help you single out those who are in favor of you. Considering that people can be pretty complex, your capability to understand their true persona cannot be overstated. For instance, if you're pursuing a career that involves serving the public, you will find yourself surrounded by all sorts of people. Clearly, not all of those people wish you well. Nevertheless, in the same breath, not all of them are against you. In such a situation, you have to exercise a lot of care, lest you end up working with your enemy who will eventually bring you down. If you tell your secrets to the enemy, he will run out there and spill it all. If you get close enough to the enemy, he might sow bad thoughts into your mind, which will see you taking the wrong direction. All of these can be avoided by sharpening your capability to tell good people apart from bad people. Of course, this is not a skill you can develop overnight. You have to practice repeatedly until you are good at spotting the fake ones.

It helps avoid conflict

In most cases, conflict arises because of a disparity in expectations. In a relationship, if the man expects one thing from his mate, and his wish is never met, it can cause him grief. And the vice versa is true. These are the kind of scenarios that cause conflict in a relationship. If the man had taken the time to understand what their partner is really like, they would not be shocked at a later time, when their partner behaved a certain way. Thus, it is important to understand the person that you're getting into a relationship with, for this will minimize your fights. Analyzing a person helps you understand their triggers. You get an opportunity to decide whether or not you want to involve yourself with them. If you're looking for a life partner, there are some things that you cannot compromise on, and so you must analyze potential candidates to find out whether or not they possess these characteristics. If you ignore this step, you are at risk of having a tumultuous marriage. Understanding what other people's personalities are like is a form of educating yourself on how to act or not act in front of these people. When you learn that someone is not into corny jokes, you will stop yourself from acting in a corny way, and in the same breath, when you realize that someone has a very fun attitude, you will try not to be a bore.

It allows you to appreciate diversity

Human beings are incredibly diverse. And this is a good thing. You cannot really understand this diversity until you pay attention to other people. Someone who comes from Asia might exhibit certain personality traits that differ from the average American. This is not a chance to bash the Asian for being different than you, but rather, it is an opportunity to appreciate the uniqueness of the Asian. People who bash others for being different than them are simply narrow-minded. Analyzing people gives you the power to recognize and accept our differences. It makes you a more cultured person. If you travel to other parts of the world, you will easily fit in because you have a mindset of adjusting. On the other hand, someone who is opposed to the recognition and appreciation of diversity will find himself at loggerheads with people who are unlike him.

It helps you fine-tune your goals

We don't live in a vacuum. The actions, words, and behaviors of other people will affect us. Every person has an idol that they look up to. Your idol is the person that you would want to trade lives with. Apart from giving you hope; your role model gives you an opportunity to study the various qualities you will require in that line of work. For instance, if you want to become a journalist, you must know that it is not just about having language skills, but you must improve your personality, so that more people will not only be comfortable around you, enough to open up and let out their secrets. When you take on the practice of keenly observing other people, you are in a position to determine which career path suits your qualities.

It helps you understand the motivations of people

At the end of the day, there's a motive behind every action, but these motives are not always obvious. Some people will instantly reveal who they are, but there are people who will try to downplay their real image. But if you're a good observer, you can always tell what is going on. By taking your time to analyze people, you are in a much better position to understand what their goals are. Having this knowledge helps you take self-preserving decisions. Manipulative people are known for acting or speaking in a way that won't betray their manipulative agenda. Unless you are extra careful in your analysis of their persona, you might miss their motive, and become another one of their victims.

It helps you understand a person's strengths

Every human being has both weaknesses and strengths. The reason why some of us become successful is that we capitalize on our strengths. Failure to capitalize on our strengths can make us feel disillusioned about life. The skill of identifying our strengths is important in identifying other people's strengths. Thus, when you are looking for someone to work with, you will be in a position to identify their strengths and weaknesses, which will make your team of high quality.

It helps in predicting behavior

Your capability to analyze personalities is vital in predicting how various people will act under different circumstances. Life is not one smooth ride. There are many challenges encountered on the road. In addition, for the most part, success depends on how we handle challenges. Being able to analyze various personalities empowers you to understand how people will react to challenges. For instance, if you notice that someone has the markings of a violent personality, or has anger issues, you might want to skip on that person because their violent nature will become soon apparent.

Chapter 2 - How To Analyze People Using Dark Psychology?

While some people use dark psychology tactics specifically to hurt and harm the intended target, there are many of us who use it without even being aware that we are manipulating the workings of other people's minds. These tactics are intentionally and/or unintentionally imbibed into our system through various means including:

• During our childhood from seeing how adults, especially parents, behaved

• During our adolescence as our minds and our ability to understand behaviors grew and expanded

• Watching others succeed with the use of these tactics

• Using a tactic unintentionally initially but when it worked to get their desires, beginning to use it intentionally

• Some people (like salespeople, public speakers, politicians, etc.) are actually trained to use these dark tactics to achieve their ends

The detail as to how these dark psychologies are used in our daily lives and later on we can see how there are some people who use it deliberately and with an intention to harm or cheat or gain undue advantages.

Commonly Used Dark Psychology Tactics

Love flooding – Complimenting, praising, and buttering people up to get them to follow your command and/or comply with your request

Lying – Giving untrue versions of happenings, exaggerating, giving partial truths, etc. to get your bidding done.

Love Denial – Withholding love and affection until you get what you want from your loved ones

Withdrawal – Giving the silent treatment or avoiding the person until your requests and needs are served

Restricting choices – Giving people access to choices that will distract them from the other choices that you do not want them to make

Semantic Manipulation – This is a very powerful technique where the manipulator uses commonly known words with accepted meanings during a conversation but later on chooses to say that he or she meant something different when using that particular word. This new meaning could change the entire definition of the word(s) involved and could steer the outcome of the conversation to what the manipulator wanted.

Reverse Psychology – Telling someone to do something in a particular way so that they will do the opposite, which is exactly what you want them to do.

Deliberate Use of Dark Tactics

Here is a small list of people who use dark psychology tactics in a deliberate way

Narcissists – People clinically diagnosed with narcissism have a bloated sense of self-worth and they are compelled by a need to make others believe that they are superior. In order to realize their deep desires of being adored and worshipped by everybody, narcissists are commonly known to use dark psychology and unethical persuasive tactics.

Sociopaths – Clinically diagnosed sociopaths are persuasive, intelligent, and charming too. However, they lack emotion and they feel no remorse because of which they do not hesitate to use dark psychology tactics to create superficial relationships with others and then take undue advantage of these people.

Attorneys – Driven by a deep passion to win each and every case under their care, attorneys, very often, use dark psychology tactics to get their desired outcomes.

Politicians – Using dark psychology tactics, politicians convince people to cast votes in their favor by convincing them that their view is the perfect view.

Sales People – This set of people are so focused on achieving their sales numbers that they do not think twice about manipulating people using dark persuasion and other unethical tactics to convince people of their dire need for a product or service they are selling.

Leaders – There are many leaders who use dark psychology techniques to get their subordinates and team members to comply more, to work harder or to perform better, etc.

Public Speakers – There are public speakers that can use dark tactics to heighten the emotional state of a large audience knowing fully well that it will lead to bigger backroom sales for the products and services they are offering.

Selfish People – This could be anyone who always puts his or her needs above everyone else's. They are willing to let others forego their benefits so that they themselves are benefited. They have no problem with win-lose outcomes where they win and others lose.

This list make you aware of such people who can manipulate you to do things that you don't want to do and the second one is to help you with self-realization. Are you using tactics that these people use to get what you want? How then can you discern between ethical tactics and dark ones so that there is good for all stakeholders? Also, knowing about these dark psychology tactics and the people who are most prone to using them will put you on guard and make you realize if anyone is using them to cause you harm.

Using dark tactics might work in the short-term but is bound to boomerang cruelly on you and affect elements such as sustainable business practices, employee and/or customer loyalty and sustainable profits negatively.

The question to ask yourself is this: Is what I am doing of help to the other person? Yes, it can help you too. However, the other person is more important in this realm. If it is solely for your own benefit, then you are definitely using dark tactics. If you can clearly see the good for the other person, then it easily falls into ethical persuasion tactics.

- Why do I want to use the technique? Who benefits from it and how?
- Do I feel good about the approach I am taking?
- Is there total transparency and honesty in the transaction?
- Will the other person get long-term benefits from this transaction?
- Will there be more trust between me and the other person when this transaction gets completed?

The answers to the above question are critical in determining whether a dark psychology tactic will result in a win-win situation. A mutually win-win situation is what the intention should be to clearly know whether the use of dark tactics is good or not.

So, again, you can see it is so easy to manipulate and be manipulated depending on which side of the power equation you are on. This is also meant to help you understand and reassess what your own standing is on the use of dark psychology in your life including in the realms of your profession, your leadership, your personal relationships, parenting, and all other forms of relationships.

Use of Dark Psychology in the Online Mode

In today's Internet-powered world, this chapter will be left half done if I do not mention the use of the Internet by unscrupulous individuals to draw victims and cause harm using dark psychology tactics. Cyber-stealth is a common criminal activity that law enforcement agencies are grappling to keep under control.

Ease of Deception – It is very easy to deceive people online driven by the veil of anonymity that the Internet provides. Stealth and camouflage are the primary survival instincts of all living beings and unscrupulous people will find it very tempting use these instincts to victimize through the Internet.

No access to the physical person – This enhances the ease of deception as the victim cannot see or read the nonverbal aspects of the communication including body language, facial features, etc.

The most confounding part of online deception is the fact that victims are fully aware that there could be something wrong taking place here and yet, they do not hesitate to take the plunge.

Understanding the human Face

Reading the eyes

Power gaze- this happens during social interactions, like interviews, where one person (usually in the power position) is assessing the person they're speaking to. This will usually take the form of someone looking back and forth between your eyes and forehead, making a small triangle with their eyes.

Social gaze- this happens between people who know each other well and have a close relationship. They will look from eye to eye, then the lips. However, their eyes may occasionally dart across other parts of the face, but the triangle will still appear.

Intimate gaze- this happens between two people who are very close or have just had an encounter that made them feel extremely close. The eyes will dart back and forth between the eyes and then down at the chest, not necessarily the breast, although that does also happen.

Blinking- this can be a sign of nerves, and potentially deception, if it happens in with a higher than normal frequency. Reduced blinking may also be a sign that someone is aware of their blinking and are trying to control it.

Pupils- the pupils are a great way to see what, or who, someone may want since the pupils tend to dilate when we look at something we want. This happens so that the eye can take in more light and see better.

Eye blocking- this is usually a sign that someone is uninterested or unimpressed and simply doesn't want to keep looking at someone or something. Seeing someone rubbing their eyes hiding them while you're talking is usually not a good sign.

Mouth;

Pursed lips- this can point to someone feeling distaste, distrust or disapproval during a certain interaction. This can happen for less than a second, but can be useful to remember for reading some people.

Lip biting- this is normally a sign that someone is nervous, stressed or anxious. Another time someone may do this is if they are aroused.

Movement

Mirroring- this is a good way to see if someone is fully engaged in an interaction or not. Mirroring usually happens when we are around people we admire, trust or like. Consider changing your posture or using a certain small action, like slightly shifting your weight, to see if someone copies you.

Head nodding- people can nod fast when they are patiently listening to someone. However, fast nodding is usually a sign that someone is eager to start talking themselves or simply leave as fast as they can.

Head shaking- shaking the head side-to-side can happen when people disagree or are in disbelief of something. This is said to be one of those expressions that formed by how we learn to refuse food we as infants.

Head tilting- someone tilting their head to the side is often done when someone is listening intently. Tilting the head back, however, can be a sign of suspicion or uncertainty.

Chapter 3 - Understanding Intentions

If we had the definite guide to spot a romantic interest, Tinder would go broke. That said, it is not hard to identify the telltale signs if someone is interested in you. Granted that some people are oblivious to it—but if you really do focus, you'd come to the realization if that person is indeed romantically interested in you or if they are just being flirtatious.

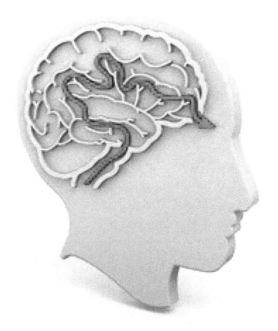

How to decode if someone is interested in you sentimentally

Usually, that special someone starts with a casual acquaintance, which leads to friendship—and before you know it, you look at this friend in a different light and keep thinking about them. Do they feel the same way you feel? Identifying if someone is interested in you romantically requires the careful and skillful interpretation of signals and actions.

Ways to Figure Out If Someone Is Romantically Interested

Here are 15 ways to figure out if someone is romantically interested in you or if they are just flirting for the thrill of it:

1. THEIR CONVERSATIONS with you

CONVERSATIONS, meaningful ones, are one of the ways a person shows a deeper interest in you and what you do. Do they keep asking you questions in an attempt to keep the conversation going? Pay attention to the questions they ask because it can tell you if they are genuinely showing interest in the things you do and like. A good and long conversation about your likes, dislikes, favorite music, and so on is a classic sign of someone genuinely liking you and your company. If you are enjoying the conversation and the other person is engaging in it without looking bored or yawning, this is a sign that both parties are equally interested in each other.

2 THEY KEEP bumping into you.

CALL it fate but this can also be a sign that they like you and they are engineering any possible opportunities to meet you. This is sweet but can also be creepy if it becomes too much like stalking. If you feel that this person is following you or you suddenly feel uncomfortable, listen to your gut feeling and make a report. Stalking is serious and dangerous. However, if bumping into you happens to be at places like the cafeteria or the lunchroom or neighborhood coffee place and not specific places like your gym that you've been going to for years, your house or anyway specific and private – make a complaint.

3 They discuss future plans.

Another sign that someone could be romantically interested in you is if they plan for more dates or start talking about the near future because they clearly see you in it. It isn't about plans of getting married or buying a house but merely simple things like a concert in your area that they'd like to take you to or even a friend's party in a week's time that they'd like you to come with. They have these upcoming events and they'd like you to be part of it.

4 Five more minutes

If someone is interested in you, chances are they would like to spend a few more minutes with you. They don't mind adjusting their schedule just so they can spend an extra 5 more minutes to talk to you or even spend that extra 5 minutes on the phone just so they can continue talking to you. The fact that they do this is also an indication that they have romantic feelings for you.

5 Reasons to spend time together

'I'm in the area—want to grab a bite?' or, 'Oh you're having a cold? I can make a mean chicken soup—I'll bring it over' or even 'What are you doing right now? Want to go have dinner together?' Make no mistake that these could just be that the person likes spending time with you simply because you are a cool person to hang out with but if these reasons keep piling up and it only involves just the two of you, it is probably a big sign that this person likes you.

6 Observe their body language.

If someone likes you, they mirror your body language and your movements. They sit in closer, they lean in, they smile when you smile, they find ways to touch you (not in a creepy way) like brushing against your shoulder, putting a strand of your hair behind your ear – all these are classic flirtation signs and, if you are uncomfortable, say so but if you are enjoying it, this person is clearly into you.

7 The compliments are mountainous.

Complimenting someone excessively can be a sign of ass-kissing or just trying to be nice. But if this person compliments you sincerely, it could be that they are interested in you. Look out for verbal cues such as complimenting your fashion choice or the way you style your hair. It could be that they are just being friendly, but them dropping compliments every time you meet is a big sign of them being interested in you.

8 They remember the little things.

THE CLOSER YOU get to know someone, the more information you divulge to them. Your romantic interest will pick up a lot of interesting things about you and save it in their long-term memory and these things can be your favorite color, your favorite ice cream flavor, the first movie you watched together, where you first met – all of this is an indication that this person is genuinely interested in you.

9 Conversation Starters

SOME PEOPLE ARE shy and are not big talkers so while this is something to take note of, you cannot be the only one initiating contact all the time. If someone is willing to connect despite them being shy, that means they really do want to talk to you. Having one-way initiations for everything is a definite NO that the other person doesn't like you and do not see the need to spend the time to talk or even meet you, but if they initiate contact as much as you do, that is a sure sign that they are into you.

10 Other People Are Off-Limits.

TAKE note of when a person talks about someone else—do they talk a lot about other girls or guys when they are with you? Or is the conversation focused on just you and your person? What a person says in a conversation and how they refer to other people in their social circle can give you real clues into whether they are romantically interested in you. Talking about going on a date with a girl or guy is not really a good indication that this person likes you.

TRUSTING your feelings and your intuitions in all these possible scenarios above is the best bet. Remember that different people do different things to show someone they care or that they are interested in them and cultural values, upbringing, and societal norms also play a big part in identifying these signs, so nothing is set in stone. All the signs described above are a good telling sign that a person is interested in you especially if they like spending more and more time with you. Even if you are not sure, you can exhibit signs that you are interested in them so that they will also have an idea but to be on the safe side, telling someone that you like them, and you'd like to get to know them better and even start dating is the best way forward to prevent any miscommunication or misunderstanding between two people.

OF COURSE, the game of love is not as straightforward and as simple as that. It takes a little bit of dating experience to figure out if someone is into you or not or you can just do the good old fashioned trial and error, get your heart broken, kiss all the toads until you meet your prince or princess charming.

Never let yourself be surprised by a lie

Most of the lies people tell are undetected. This happens because other than the fact that many people don't know how to deal with liars, they don't know how to read them in the first place. Some people don't care or don't think the lie is something worth causing a fuss about. Think about the number of lies you told your parents when you were growing up, for example. If you remember correctly, none of that will fly by you if your kids tried it on you today. How come your parents let you off easily?

The example above is about very simple lies, which, in most cases, cause no harm. However, some lies have far-reaching effects, and if you don't deal with them when you should, they form a recipe for disaster. When you keep getting away with lies, a pattern forms, and as time goes by, you embrace lies as the best option to deal with everything.

What do you do with lies? How do you deal with a liar in your life? Perhaps this is someone so close to you that you cannot get rid of them, but you can stand them somehow. The following are useful tips that will help you learn how to handle the situation better:

Prioritize Personal Safety. Your safety is more important than anything else. Even if you want to save the relationship, it means nothing if you cannot enjoy the results. Before you confront someone about their lies, always make sure you are safe. Scan the environment and ensure no harm can befall you.

You can never be too sure what the nature of the confrontation will be or what it might spiral into. Because of this, it is safe to bring someone else as a buffer, just in case things get out of hand. This is true because, many times, when people are confronted about their lies, they can be aggressive to scare you off and drop the issue altogether.

Differentiate Lies from the Truth. It might not be easy to read so much into someone's words, but you can tell so much from their body language. This is a good opportunity for you to tell the difference between the truth and the lies. Awareness of some of the symptoms you are being lied to can help you identify some pointers that someone is not honest with you. You need to be conscious of their behavioral patterns.

Exit the Situation. You cannot solve everything at the same time. In some confrontations, it is better if you know the right time to remove yourself from the equation. When you realize that things are getting heated, you have to take a step back and evaluate your position from afar.

If the relationship you share with the person you are confronting means anything to both or either of you, cooling off will allow you both to reflect on what has been said, and by the time you get back to discussing it again, you might have a better chance of handling the matter well.

Remember that even if you exit the situation and get back to it later, it might be a while before the liar stops lying completely. Some people never do. They just chose the people they lie to and those they stay true to. With this in mind, remember that if you decide to stay and keep them by your side, this is a journey that might take a very long time, and you might need to seek professional help. You should also notice whether they are willing to change or not. It is pointless trying to change someone who has no intention to do so.

Empathize. In as much as you are trying to understand and deal with a liar, remember that something is wrong with them, so you should empathize. There might be several reasons why they choose lies over the truth. Show them that you understand, especially if you know their lies are a self-defense mechanism.

Many compulsive liars need professional help. When it comes to empathy, in some cases, you don't even need to talk. Just be there for them and listen. As much as it is painful for you to see them go through this experience, it is also the right thing to do. Do not judge. Listen to them. Explain their reasons. If you realize they are lying about that too, call them out on it and implore them to take your concern seriously. At some point, they will have to come clean.

Identify the Type of Lies. People tell different kinds of lies. While some lays cause destruction and pain, some lies are just harmless. It would be ideal if you learned how to identify the difference between a harmless lie and a nefarious lie.

Of course, we contend that it is not okay to lie, but at times, it is inevitable. If you can tell the difference between these two situations, you are in a better position because you can determine how to handle the situation going forward.

For a white lie, while it might be harmless, don't forget to remind the liar that you know what they did. Warn them of consequences and remind them that they will not get away with it next time. It is unsafe to ignore such lies because if they get used to it, there can only be one outcome, and it's not a great one.

Ask for Help. You know them better than anyone else, so there is a good chance you might need help in handling the confrontation. Get help. Bring in professionals or other family members that you believe can help you handle the situation better.

Introducing someone else into the picture provides a third-party perspective, which provides common ground for all of you. Remember that if you are bringing in a third party, it should not be someone that intimidates the person you are confronting. Otherwise, they can choose to box their feelings and ignore the issue altogether.

Stay Calm. You need to stay calm whenever you are confronting a liar. Remember that you hold power in this conversation since you confronted them about it. Try not to lose your nerves because you might end up in an argument that will not solve anything.

Explain to them in the best way possible what their lies have done to your life, your relationship with them, and more importantly, trust between the two of you. Unless they are willing to put in the work and repair the damage, remind them that there will be consequences, and state them clearly.

As you confront them about the lies, remember that you need to keep the situation calm and welcoming so that they don't feel like you are ganging up on them or they are being ambushed. However much you feel they hurt you, yours is the voice of reason, so try to keep it calm.

Healthy Confrontation. Confronting a liar is not easy, especially for someone close to you. However, some part of their mind knows this, and they know how much you struggle to bring yourself to confront them. There is always a good way to confront someone about their lies.

First, make sure you do it in private. Never confront them in public because this only shames them. Before the confrontation, ensure you have sufficient evidence to back your claims. Pathological liars are performers, so you can expect that they will resist and try to play it out as something else. They might even insist you are out to harm them. However, you must be steadfast because you are doing this for the greater good, which is to help them.

Always Keep Evidence. At times the easiest way to help someone is to confront them in the most painful way— to expose them. You have to be careful about this because exposure can backfire if not done properly. A lot of people have suffered irreparable differences and never made up. The first thing you should do if you are to expose a liar is to ensure the environment is convenient. If you have to do it in front of people, do it in the presence of people who care for them, who are willing to support them if they are willing to change. From the moment you discover their lies, gather as much evidence as possible. Document it if possible so that it is congruent with the story and will help prevent loopholes in their argument. Remember that the idea is not just about exposing them and shaming them in the process. It is about exposing them to make them realize their mistakes and encourage them to change their lives for the better. It is possible. You have to find a way to do it kindly without making them feel like they are outcasts. This is important because some habitual liars already struggle with mental conditions that make them feel they are different. Singling them out aimlessly might be counter-effective if not done properly.

Determine the Subject of Interest. Habitual liars might lie all the time, but if you are keen, you can identify a pattern in their lies. There is always something that triggers them to lie; especially something they feel closely and deeply about. More often, this happens because they are afraid of confronting the truth about their lives. In this case, lying becomes their go-to mechanism whenever they feel threatened or if their position on the matter is challenged.

Repetitive patterns indicate a systemic problem, which means whatever is bothering them about the subject is deeply rooted in their minds, and it would be advisable to seek professional help. If it is not a serious concern, perhaps it might be better to leave things as they are, and instead of giving them an opportunity to lie, you can beat them to their game and change the subject to something else.

In conclusion, one of the most important things you must understand is that lies are different and they depend on the kind of situation. Liars are triggered by different things in their environment. Just as much as every lie is different, so is the lie detection mechanism. There is no one-size-fits-all method in detecting or dealing with liars. More often, two things are almost always constant—your awareness of the situation and the context. If you can perfect these two, you can easily master other skills and learn how to identify liars by recognizing the verbal and nonverbal cues and other traits.

Chapter 4 - Analyzing Cognitive Functions

Cognitive functions are defined as mental activities that involve knowledge, reasoning, memory, language, and other information that are used to make decisions in our lives and for the purpose of communication. We use what we learn to achieve tasks in life, such as making decisions, budgeting our finances, translating from one language to another and/or finding the reason(s) and/or purpose(s) behind something. How we acquire information, process it, and use it later is vital to our development and communication with others. It can also be heavily influenced by our relationships with other people, places, and situations.

There are several ways in which our mind acquires and absorbs new information:

Extraverted Sensing

This refers to how we acquire information through our five senses (taste, smell, sight, hearing, and touch) and how these experiences are translated into our mind to retain and develop this information. When we taste a new food or observe a new species of animal, it becomes a learning experience that we acquire and "file" in our mind for future reference and knowledge.

Introverted Sensing

This refers to recalling a previous experience as it was remembered. This new scent of a flower discovered a week before, or the sound of someone's voice you recently met at a conference. The more impactful or unique the experience, the more likely you are to remember and recall the event, person, or item more vividly.

Extraverted Thinking

This is a process where we make a judgment or decision based on external facts or items that we take into consideration. An example would be making a quick judgment immediately following a vehicular accident, that involves contacting an emergency without hesitation. This is a quick or "snap" decision based on external information available at the time. In cases where there is an imminent danger or appears to be a threat (an upcoming natural disaster or fire), the decision to vacate, then make other plans is part of the extraverted thinking process. These choices are made based on objective, external facts that may impact our emotions, though they require only observation in order to determine the next step(s) and decision(s) to make.

Introverted Thinking

This decision-making process is based on internal, personal needs and values, as opposed to external, objective items. Often, judgments or choices made through introverted thinking tend to be more emotionally based and personal in nature and may or may not consider external factors. An example would be to abruptly leave a room or conversation when someone makes an offensive joke or comment or to respond with an objection if the comment has a personal impact.

How we process, retain, and use information that we acquire varies depending on how we perceive and remember it. This process also impacts how we communicate with other people and how they read our verbal and non-verbal cues.

It's important to become familiar with different types of communication, as these can serve as a "window" into understanding more about how we are perceived and how we communicate with others.

Verbal Communication

The way we express ourselves verbally to another person or within a group is the most common form of communication. How we speak to other people and how they communicate with us has an impact on our response and perception. While non-verbal cues and communication are important to understand, there are elements to a verbal expression that is equally vital to become familiar with:

A person's tone, emphasis, or lack of emphasis on certain words, phrases, and speech can vary widely depending on their intentions. For example, a simple phrase may seem uneventful or unimportant if spoken in a monotone or unenthusiastic tone of voice. If the person is known for making sarcastic remarks or statements, a dull expression may indicate sarcasm or simply a lack of interest. If the same phrase or statement is spoken with more enthusiasm or excitement, it may generate more attention and an equally excited response. Sometimes it's not what we say, but rather how we say it.

The volume and speed at which we talk and be an indicator of our mood or attitude surrounding a specific topic or event. For example, if we state "I have to go to school" in a slow, quiet and monotone voice, it may signify boredom or displeasure in attending school.

On the other hand, if we make the statement with more cheer and express it loudly, it may indicate something more positive. Speaking quickly and stumbling over words may indicate nervousness or fear, whereas speaking loudly with a deliberate tone may denote anger or frustration.

Verbal sounds, such as sighing, laughter, pausing or using "filler" words such as "umm" or "uh" can indicate a variety of different moods or impressions.

Pausing during a sentence or conversation may be a sign thinking before you speak, or simply "searching" for the right words or description to use as a response.

Sighing can be a sign of frustration, despair, or grief. It can also indicate being tired and not wanting to talk any further. Laughter usually indicates a light-hearted or humorous comment, or it can indicate nervousness. Some people will use laughter to convince others that they are happier or more content, whether that is the case or not.

The style of verbal communication can indicate a lot about how a person feels. Interpreting verbal cues or changes in speech patterns or mood can signal when it is appropriate to respond, how to respond, and when merely leaving the conversation is the best option. For example, if a person sounds nervous or anxious, providing comforting words and encouragement may be appropriate. If someone sighs or shows signs of frustration, asking them if they need assistance or simply giving them space for reflection can be a useful way to communicate.

Facial Expressions

Facial expressions and gestures are an essential means of understanding what people mean to say and how even when they may not verbalize their innermost thoughts and ideas. Most facial gestures or movements are easy to understand and require little or no explanation. If a good friend or family member smile upon meeting with you, they are displaying joy and contentment. During a tragic event or mourning a loss, people may display a somber expression of sadness. Other emotions and experiences can trigger many different facial expressions, and some are more obvious than others. In cases where a person is confronted with making a decision or asked if they accept or agree with a certain rule or decision, they may state "yes, sure," yet frown at the same time. These two concurrent, yet conflicting lines of communication can mean that the person wants you to believe that he or she is in agreement, but their facial expression indicates they do not agree.

Sometimes, facial expressions are obvious and other types they can be contrary or opposite to what a person may say. Examples of communication through facial gestures or expressions often convey true emotions, including fear, anger, sadness, confusion, excitement, shock, and happiness. If a person's facial expression matches how we perceive them or how they speak, we tend to trust them because they are showing consistent or "true" feelings.

In several studies conducted on the impact of facial expressions and their impact on other people, it was noted that more people recognized happier, joyful expressions as being more confident and intelligent, whereas angry, frustrated expressions were not valued as highly. Some people may use a smile or friendly face to mask true feelings of sadness or anger so that they are not perceived as they truly feel.

Eye Reading

Eye movements, gazing, or avoiding contact are examples of communication.

Eye expressions are often used with other facial gestures to show a variety of emotions or reactions. They can also indicate whether a person is paying close attention if they are interested in what you have to say, or whether they prefer to avoid the conversation altogether. In studying the various types of eye expressions or movements, we can gain a better understanding of how they communicate with us:

If a person maintains consistent eye contact with a continuous gaze, they are likely interested in you and what you have to say or offer.

If you maintain eye contact with someone, they will likely "read" this gesture as a show of interest and attention. People respond well to attention and will often go to great lengths to maintain it once they have your undivided attention.

Avoiding eye contact and/or frequently looking away is a sign of disinterest or boredom in a topic or person. If you have to continuously remind someone to notice you or speak louder or more enthusiastically to hold another person's attention, it's likely because you've noticed a lack of interest. They may dart their eyes away from you and look elsewhere. If they are tired or overworked, it may simply mean that they don't possess the energy to pay attention at the moment, though they may show more interest at another time. Another reason for avoiding eye contact may occur when someone feels embarrassed, uncomfortable, or attempting to hide their true feelings or thoughts on a topic or situation. While some people are eager to debate or challenge a subject, many people prefer to avoid the discussion altogether. They may not express this verbally, though their lack of eye contact is a sure sign of avoidance.

Blinking may be a sign of excitement or nervousness. Some people may often blink or on occasion. They may not even be aware of it, as it is a normal function that occurs whether we realize it or not. In situations where a person may be overtired or bored, they may purposely blink to keep their focus. Blinking may also be a habit or circumstantial and have not related to expression or communication at all sometimes.

Eye rolling or making deliberate movements in direct response to a joke or comment are other examples of eye expressions. They are usually specific in nature, such as responding to a silly joke with eye-rolling or closing your eyes momentarily to show displeasure or disagreement with a statement or opinion.

In addition to eye expressions, facial movements, and verbal cues, there are many other verbal and non-verbal signs that can give us an indication of someone's true feelings or intentions. Examples of hand gestures, postures, and other non-verbal motions are described in more detail below:

Hand Gestures

The way we gesture with our hands, arms, and fingers can show enthusiasm or excitement about a specific topic in general. There are specific movements and symbols or signs we make that can be more indicative of something we want, request, or to show approval. One simple gesture of the fingers or sway of the hand can mean the difference between dismissal and approval. Other movements are habitual and maybe a specific characteristic of a person's mannerisms as well: Fingers are often used to communicate in a quick and simple way, especially when verbalizing isn't an option (due to a long-distance or busy crowd), and a clear sign is needed. For example, giving a "thumbs up" is a sign of approval or agreement. It may also confirm that everything is in order and "good." "Thumbs down" can indicate failure or disappointment. Pointing fingers can be an accusatory action and used to aim or point at someone to blame them for action. This gesture can also be used, in some cases, for emphasis or as a way to describe a situation or scenario while keeping your attention. In most cases, finger-pointing is considered rude and even obscene. It can make someone feel targeted or humiliated and should be avoided.

An upward "V" was used as a sign of peace in the 1960s or as a symbol of victory. Forming a circle with the index and thumb, with the remaining fingers spread indicates everything is "ok." It's also a signal that a plan or event is in good order. It can also symbolize perfection. To curl your index finger towards someone can summon them. One of the most positive finger symbols worldwide is the crossing of the index and middle finger. This indicates good fortune and luck. In some countries or regions, these and other hand signs could be interpreted as something negative, such as an insult or lewd comment.

It's always a good idea to research hand gestures and other customs before traveling, to ensure appropriate and respectful communication is used.

A flat hand will often mean "stop" or stay back, to limit contact with someone or signal for them to cease acting or behaving in a certain way. This sign can similarly mean "stay" or to hold a specific thought or position. It can also translate into "talk to the hand," which basically indicates a lack of interest in communicating with someone, therefore, using your hand as a barrier. In some cultures, this hand sign can indicate reassurance, or as a way to summon or ask someone for their assistance.

Body Posture

Our posture and how we pose can give away our innermost thoughts and insecurities. When a person is often slouching forward and looking downward, it's a symptom of shame or a lack of self-confidence. It may be a pose or position that we don't intend to portray, as it may reveal certain feelings of insecurity or weaknesses that we would rather hide.

When a person sits or stands with their arms open and with a straight, upright posture, it shows engagement and confidence when they speak or listen. They are interested in what the other person or people have to say and want to contribute. Some people may go further to lean forward to acknowledge when someone makes a comment.

Signs of avoidance, tension or feeling defensive are often conveyed through body language and a variety of poses and positions, including sitting with arms folded across the chest with a stern facial expression or none at all.

In this position, the upper body may be turned away from the person communicating to indicate their disapproval or a clear message of having no interest in reciprocating. In a standing position, a person showing avoidance may simply walk away, usually with their arms folded and all forms of contact, with their eyes or face are minimized as much as possible. Other signs of avoidance or limiting contact may include fidgeting, looking away, or gazing in another direction to display a clear message of disinterest.

Displaying confidence and a willingness to communicate is often shown with open gestures that symbolize and an invitation to talk or share discussion. In this situation, the posture is confident, and hands are usually used minimally unless gesturing to supplement the description of a situation or item.

When people display a confident, upright posture with direct eye contact and a firm but a friendly disposition, they are more likely to grab your attention and keep you listening. Some people are natural with social engagement, while others practice these techniques to improve their performance in business, networking, and sales.

Head Movements

Nodding, shaking from side to side or tilting to one side are all examples of head movements that convey a certain feeling or emotion. Tilting the head to one side is a way of saying, "I'm interested and want to know more." When someone displays this action, it usually means they want to listen to you and are interested in what you have to say. In some cases, it can be a sign that feels attraction towards you, and for this reason, they want to know more about you. In some situations, where a person is observing an event or piece of artwork, they may tilt their head when they are trying to understand or interpret its meaning or message. This may occur when the image or item is complex or enigmatic, and tilting your head to adjust the gaze or perspective can provide more options for viewing and understanding.

Tilting the head upwards to extend the chin is a show of dominance or feel above other people. It can also indicate a strong sense of confidence in leadership. It's often used by executives and politicians when they speak to a crowd or group. This gesture can also be read as a form of arrogance or superiority, which may effectively hide any insecurity and convey a sense of fearlessness. On the contrary, by tilting the head and chin downward, this could mean rejection, bashfulness, or a sense of shame. It also indicates a lack of confidence and can make others see you as more sensitive to criticism. Facing forward with your chin pushed inward indicates a defensive gesture or a sign that someone feels threatened by a new event, situation, or change. This gesture may spontaneously occur when another person "steals" the spotlight from someone else.

Nodding of the head is a common non-verbal way of saying "yes" or "I agree" with someone. If done quickly and anxiously, a quick nod may indicate a strong eagerness to agree and coincide with another person's comments and ideas. Shaking the head from side to side is usually the opposite of nodding, indicating a "no" or non-approval.

Playfully tossing the head from one side to another during a casual conversation may indicate signs of attraction towards someone in the group. It also displays a measure of comfort and willingness to submit and engage on a more personal level.

Handwriting

The way people write says a lot about their personality and how they express themselves. Often, people tend to use texting and online communication as their main source of written expression, though handwriting still remains important for taking notes, signing paperwork and adding a personal touch or expression to a card or letter. The most common use of handwriting, especially in business, is a signature. The formation of letters, their spacing, and size are factors taken into consideration when analyzing a person through their handwriting:

Letters spaced apart and written in a medium to large size can indicate a sense of freedom and sincerity. This may also indicate a tendency towards being more generous and sharing, and a sense of independence and a free-spirited attitude.

Letters or words that were written closely together may indicate that a person is not aware of personal space or boundaries and may be intrusive or step over the line sometimes.

Printing lightly with a pen or pencil indicates a degree of sensitivity and care, whereas a heavier hand can mean a more tense and angry attitude. An evenly, moderately printing pressure is ideal, as it can indicate a level of consistency and commitment in the writer

Some signatures are clear and easy to read, whereas others may appear like a scribble or illegible. People who sign with a deliberately clear print or handwriting are easier to understand and desire to be understood.

They tend to be straight-forward and an "open book." People who use messy or less legible styles of signatures tend to be more private and concealed.

The way t's are crossed, I's are dotted, and other letters are formed also provide ways in which we read other people by their writing habits.

Some analysis of even seemingly insignificant styles in writing, such as how closely an "I" is dotted to the openness or closed loop of a lowercase "l" can seem trivial, though they are all signs of specific personality types and practices. For example, when an "I" is closely dotted, this may indicate an organized mind and lifestyle. Dots over an "I" or "j" that are more playful, such as a circle or heart, may be interpreted as creative and inventive. If a person crosses their "t" high, they may have a goal-oriented way of living, where they aim high and strive for greatness, whereas crossing a "t" low or barely at all may be a lack of ambition or drive. In handwriting a lowercase "l," a large loop may show a sign of an open-mind and ready-to-learn mentality, whereas a smaller space within the loop is likely a sign of close-mindedness and stubbornness.

Round, circular letters indicate a potential for creativity and artistic talent. If letters are both round, curvy and large, this may indicate a combination of showing generosity along with a talent for the arts, with a willingness to share their talent and abilities with others for greater appreciation. Pointed, sharply written letters and words indicate a sign of intelligence and logic.

The way letters are slanted in handwriting can indicate.

Chapter 5 - Reading Thoughts?!

I believe in the ability to read other people's thoughts. I believe one hundred percent. There is nothing difficult in this, for me to read the thoughts of other people is like listening to what they say. And I do not see any mystery in this. Reading thoughts as naturally as eating or breathing. In fact, we all read the mind—only, do it unconsciously. Someone succeeds better, someone worse, someone uses this talent, and someone does not. But I'm sure we can all develop this natural ability. We know that we read our thoughts, we know how to do it, which means we can do it better. That's what this book is about. But what do I mean by "read minds"? What do I mean when I say "we do it every day unconsciously"? What is it really?

For a start, I will note what does not apply to the process of reading thoughts in my understanding. In psychology, they call "reading minds" (in plain English Mind Reading). The phenomenon is the result of which so many married couples find themselves at the reception of a psychotherapist—this happens when partners believe that one should know the thoughts of the other.

"If he really loves me, he should understand that I didn't want to go to that party. So what if I said yes? He should have known that I didn't want it. "

Or:

"He doesn't care about me since he doesn't understand how I feel."

Requiring another person to know your thoughts is the height of egocentrism. No less dangerous is a situation in which a person believes that he knows the thoughts of another, and in reality, only projects his own thoughts onto his behavior.

"No, she will hate me!"

Or:

"She smiles as if she's doing something stupid. As I thought!"

Such projection is often called the "Othello error", and we will consider it later in this book.

Descartes Error

To understand the process of "reading thoughts" and its principles, you must first define one important concept. The philosopher, mathematician, and scientist Rene Descartes, this giant of thought of the XVII century, was the author of the revolutionary transformations in the field of mathematics and Western European philosophical thought—the transformations that we still use today. Descartes died in 1650 as a result of pneumonia in Stockholm, where he arrived at the invitation of Queen Christina. Descartes had a habit peculiar to all French philosophers: to work in his warm and soft bed. The cold stone floor of a Swedish castle turned out to be a fatal test for his health. Among a number of clever thoughts, Descartes encounters many mistakes. Shortly before his death, he declared that the body and mind are different, unrelated things. It would seem that nothing could be more stupid than this statement. Of course, even at that time, there were people who understood that Descartes made a mistake, but their timid voices were drowned in violent exultation about the "genius" of the scientist. Only in our time, biologists and psychologists have been able to prove the exact opposite: that our body and our brain are inseparable from each other. However, despite the scientifically based facts, we still believe in the nonsense, spoken by Descartes. Most of us, often unconsciously, draw an invisible boundary between body and mind. To understand the content of this book, you will have to come to terms with the fact that the mind and body of a person are one, no matter how hard it is to believe. This is a scientifically proven fact.

Any thought of yours finds physical expression in your body. A thought creates an electrical impulse in brain cells that send signals to each other. Each signal has its own differences. For example, if this thought has already crossed your mind, the signal will be familiar and just repeated. A new thought involves a new constellation of brain cells, which in turn can trigger the release of hormones in the body or affect the body's autonomic nervous system, which controls the respiratory processes, pupil size, blood circulation, sweating, etc.

All thoughts somehow affect the body. Sometimes this influence is pronounced, sometimes barely noticeable. For example, when you are afraid, you experience dry mouth and blood rushes to your leg muscles so that you can flee as soon as possible. If, when you see a cashier in the supermarket, erotic fantasies arise in your head, you will immediately feel arousal in your body. Even if the physical response is difficult to notice, it is always present.

That is why, judging by the appearance, we can determine how a person feels, what he thinks and what he fears. Developing your observation abilities, you will be able to see something that you just didn't pay attention to before.

Chapter 6 - Become A Lie Detector – How To Recognize Conflicting Signals

In this chapter, I will tell you about the use of non-verbal communication in practice. There are signals that we send only in a certain situation. If you only knew what your subconscious mind is doing, it is worthwhile to find a genetically appropriate specimen (read: handsome or pretty). But before that, we will deal with another interesting problem: what happens to our subconscious when we try to lie.

A person who claims to be able to read minds and analyze others should notice when they lie to him. You have already learned to recognize the signs of falsehood and to guess from the face, whether a person is lying or telling the truth. But the most difficult thing you have to master.

The easiest way to lie is in words. We do this throughout our lives. It is harder to lie using facial expressions, although many people do it well. But the most difficult thing is to lie with your whole being (or body). We do not think about it, but the body has its own language and often says what it wants, and not what we intended. In conversation, people pay attention primarily to words, less often to facial expressions and almost never to the body of the interlocutor.

When we suspect a person of lying, we carefully listen to his words, instead of paying attention to the tone of his voice or body language. But this is the only way to check whether a person is lying or not. In fact, we see the signals of the excitement that he is experiencing (and when he lies too). He may be nervous, not because he is lying, but for another reason. There are signals that mean a lie and only a lie—and we need to learn to distinguish.

Some people are well versed in lies and its various manifestations. Others circle the finger easy. There are congenital liars for whom lying is like breathing. They do not send any signals and usually refer to psychopaths. There are people who do not know how to lie. We are all different. But most of us send signals that can be learned to distinguish.

What is a lie?

The ability to recognize lies has always been admired by people. Without this skill, it is difficult to work in the police or in court. The testimony of the classic "lie detector" is sometimes erroneous, so many scientists, including Paul Ekman, spent so much time and effort to learn to recognize a lie, and in part, they succeeded. But first, let's think about what a lie is. Most people lie all the time, or rather, their words do not quite accurately reflect reality. This is how our society and culture are organized, where lies are accepted. To the question "How are you?" The person answers "Good," he does not talk about his problems, because the other person is not interested in the interlocutor and in fact, he is just being polite.

There are situations when people are forced to lie and hide their thoughts. At a beauty contest, the winner may sob from excitement, while the losing participants are forced to smile and pretend to be happy for her. If a lie was not accepted in our society, the participants of the beauty contest would sob bitterly and something else, they would have pulled the finalist by the hair. Do not show your true feelings—this is a kind of lie.

Of course, these forms of lies do not interest us. We are interested in when people lie not out of politeness or on sociocultural motives, but on their own initiative — consciously, knowing that things that do not correspond to reality. Remember, lies are not only the lies that we speak but also the truth about which we are silent. If I say that I won a tennis match, which I actually lost, then I lie. If I say that I am having fun, but in fact I am sad, I lie.

When someone lies, he does it out of fear of punishment or in the hope of reward. Our lies always have a reason. There is also a combination of these two motives: when we want to receive an undeserved reward, but if a lie is revealed, a fine is waiting for us. For example, everyone will know that we have lied—this is also a punishment to some extent.

Conflicting Signals

A person gives false signals only when the reason becomes a very significant factor when a person risks something when he is worried. And it is the excitement that is reflected on his face—the feeling that we can read as a sign of lies. First, you need to find all the signals, and then correctly interpret them. In the case of a lie, there are always two messages: truthful and deceitful, both equally important, we must learn to distinguish between them. The message comes not only from our words but also from the whole body—all the tools that combine under the name "non-verbal communication" are used. Therefore, we are talking about how skillfully a person hides a truthful message and gives a lie for the truth. It is about self-control (that is, control over emotions and reactions). As is the case with the meaning of a facial expression, a person tries to disguise one feeling with another. To understand whether he is lying or not, you need to follow the channels of communication that are the most difficult to control. A person who speaks the truth unconsciously sends similar signals, but if we feel a symbolic discrepancy between words and facial expressions of a person or movements of his hands, then we can talk about lies. This is what I mean by "conflicting signals." We say one thing, think the other, and do the third. And the easiest way, of course, is to control your words.

American psychologist Robert Trivers came up with a solution to the problem for all professional liars. You just need to convince yourself that a lie is true. Then all of our signals, conscious and unconscious, will carry the same message.

But such manipulations of consciousness carry health risks. Inconsistent signals are often referred to as unconscious leakage or simply leakage. You may think that it's great to hide your feelings, but people are able to mask only obvious, obvious signs. Anyway, there is an unconscious leak, which is also unconsciously perceived by another person (this means that people notice this, not really aware of what they are doing). When a person lies, he cannot control all the signals that his body sends, and he will surely give himself away. But there are also pathological liars who don't betray themselves, with such you have to be especially careful. So the absence of leakage is still not a guarantee that they tell you the truth. In addition, sometimes for a leak, we can take the usual behavior of a person who is not well known. That is why it is important to note whether the signals are the result of a change in a person's normal behavior. It is necessary to carefully monitor his reactions and only then draw the appropriate conclusions.

If the interlocutor sends a number of conflicting signals, it is highly likely that he is lying. It may also mean that he is trying to hide his true feelings. Often it is easy to check. Following the methods outlined, do not forget that the signals can be sent by a person whose thoughts during your conversation are simply busy with something else. None of these methods gives an absolute guarantee. Always pay attention to the context and try not to make hasty conclusions. And in general: is it important for you if this person lying or not?

Controversial Body Language

The clearest signals are given by our nervous system. It is very difficult for us to control them. It's almost impossible to force yourself to stop sweating or blush when you worry. Unable to control pupils at the poker table. But our nervous system reacts only in the case of very strong emotions,—then what to do if a lie does not cause a person to be very excited?

Face

A person's face always expresses two states: feelings that he is ready to show to others, and his true thoughts, which he does not want to share with anyone. Sometimes these two states coincide, but this happens extremely rarely. If we try to manage our facial expressions, we do it in three ways.

• Qualification – We add to the existing facial expression another (for example, we depict a smile to hide the sadness).

• Simulation – We change the intensity of the expressions on the face, making them more or less bright. This is achieved through the activity of the facial muscles and the period of time in which they are involved.

• Falsification (simulation) – We show feelings that we really don't feel. There are other options, for example, we try not to give out our feelings (neutralization) or disguise them as others (disguise).

In order for others to believe us, we must have good control of the muscles of the face. This is especially possible for children who with pleasure "make faces" in front of a mirror. With age, this ability deteriorates, so we often have no idea how we look in a given situation. Sometimes we simply do not have time to prepare, and we do everything as if in the hope that this will "give a smooth ride".

The most difficult thing is to neutralize your feelings, to pretend that you do not feel them, especially if these feelings are strong and sincere. Often a person (against the will of a person) turns into a mask, and the interlocutor immediately realizes that there is something wrong, and tries to find out what is being hidden from him. Therefore liars prefer to mask one feeling with another. You already know that in disguise, we mainly use the lower part of the face. This means that our eyes, eyebrows, and forehead give out our true state.

Another, the most common way to disguise is a smile. Charles Darwin had a whole theory about it. He said that most often we strive to disguise negative emotions, and with a smile, there are completely different muscles that are easy to control at that moment.

A sincere smile is always symmetrical: both corners of the mouth simultaneously lift up. A fake smile may well be asymmetrical (one corner of the mouth is raised). A smile at one corner of the mouth can also speak of contempt or disgust for the interlocutor. A genuinely smiling man smiles not only with his lips but with his eyes too.

Actors, to seem sincere, try before you smile, remember something pleasant so that the joy was real. It should also be remembered that a real smile, unlike a fake one, does not appear suddenly: a person needs time to realize the joy. But to portray a lie, just one pulse.

Micro-expressions play a big role when you need to guess the state of the interlocutor. Sometimes the other person smiles and says nice things, and we feel that there is something wrong here. Most likely, our subconscious noted micro facial expressions and correctly interpreted them. The only pity is that not all people show micro-expressions or show them when they are trying to suppress emotions, and not to lie.

Eyes

They say that a liar can be recognized by the eyes. Recall the expression: "I see in your eyes that you're lying." There is a statement: if a person looks away or blinks often, he lies. Perhaps there is some truth in this. But people are so sure of this phenomenon that now that they are lying, they are trying to look their interlocutor right in the eyes. Since childhood, we have heard that a liar is afraid to look into his eyes, but unfortunately, this will not help us now. There are situations when we look to the side for natural reasons: for example, we look down, when we are sad, to the side—when we are ashamed, or we look through a person when he is unpleasant. The most experienced liars are those who can look away in time.

Excitement also gives the size of the pupils. They expand with excitement or wonder. Listen to the person and watch his pupils at the same time. If he tells you something important, his pupils cannot remain the same.

When a liar blinks, his eyes usually remain closed longer than in an honest person. The British zoologist Desmond Morris, who studied the behavior of animals and people, noticed that this happens, for example, during police interrogation. This is an unconscious human attempt to escape from reality, as does an ostrich, burying its head in the sand.

It is also important to monitor eye movements. Remember what I told you about memories and the design of new thoughts? When designing, we use our imagination, and we need it when we think about the future, create something new, invent fairy tales, and so on. Depending on whether we are remembering something or creating a new thought, our eyes move in different ways. A lie is also a construction because we are creating something that was not there. If a visual talks about something and claims that he has seen everything with his own eyes, and at the same time his gaze is directed upwards to the right, it means that he is inventing (constructing) everything. Then ask yourself: why should he invent something? For example, a person tells you: "I stayed at work and was very hungry. Then I ate pizza with Jock and immediately went home. " If at the words "I ate pizza with Jock" a person looks up to the right, then he is making it up. Something is wrong here. It is possible that he blatantly lies.

A person cannot control his view, which, while constructing, against his will, will be directed upwards to the right, which is why a liar cannot look directly into his eyes, but if a person tells you what really was the place to be, that is, he remembers, he may look you in the eye. This means that if a person had time to invent a lie, speak it to himself, maybe even memorize it, then he can calmly repeat it (remember), looking straight into your eyes. In this case, it does not matter whether he tells about a real event or all this is the fruit of his fantasy. Do not forget that not all people fit this model. It is worth thinking ten times before letting out to spend the night with an unfamiliar person, no matter what he tells you.

Arms

It is more difficult to control the face than other parts of the body because the activity of the facial muscles is associated with brain function. But we are often betrayed by other parts of the body, such as hands. Our hands can give a variety of signals. As in the case of words, a certain gesture has a certain meaning (emblem), understood by all representatives of the same culture. For example, Winston Churchill's gesture in the form of the Latin letter V, formed by two fingers, means victory, and all representatives of Western civilization know this. Lie gestures easier than ever. It is only necessary to answer the question "Did you win the match?" By lifting up two fingers. Even if in fact we brutally lost.

Sometimes we use gestures unconsciously, and they can tell us what a person really thinks and feels because he does not control them. Detecting them is not easy. Paul Ekman, for example, discovered a gesture that students made during a conversation with an unpleasant person. Unconsciously, they clenched their hands into a fist, sometimes even exposing one finger, as if showing the interviewer an indecent gesture. But this happened under the table, and this person still could not see him. There was no doubt that with a gesture the students express disgust for the interlocutor, although they do not realize that they are experiencing precisely this feeling.

Another well-known gesture is shrugging when we want to show our ignorance or that we don't care. The shoulders are raised, and, accordingly, the hands, too, palms are usually aimed at the other person.

There are also hand movements with which we illustrate our statements (for example, we outline the contours in the air, speaking of abstract concepts). All people use their hands when talking, only the activity of gestures varies from one culture to another. For example, southern Europeans—Italians and Spaniards—are very fond of accompanying their words with intensive gestures. We rarely pay attention to gestures, but in fact, they mean a lot to us.

It is impossible to communicate with a person who says one thing and shows something completely different from his hands. In my seminars, I am doing the following experiment. I look man directly in the eye, ask how much time it is, and at the same time point the finger at the window. In response, I always get: "Um ... What?", although, it would seem that there can be no simpler question. True, there are cases when the use of gestures is minimized—for example, at the moment of fatigue, when we do not have the strength or we are bored or sad, and if we focus heavily on the words of the interlocutor.

Creating new thoughts is a complex mental process. Focusing on the invention of the new, we forget about gestures. Our body is practically not involved, only the speech apparatus works. The absence of gestures is a sure sign that a person is lying. When I ask how a liar can be identified, people usually respond that he often scratches his nose. There is some truth in this. People who lie tend to hold their hands to their faces, but scratching the nose is not so common. You will be surprised, but quite often the liars cover their mouths with their hands as if they do not let the words of untruth fly from their tongues or are ashamed of what they are lying. If a person covers his mouth with his hand while talking to you, scratches his nose, constantly adjusts his glasses, tugs at the earlobe, he most likely lies.

All these gestures can sometimes be seen from someone who just sits and listens to another. Agree, we often keep silent about our true thoughts and do not speak in person to the interlocutor that, in our opinion, he lies. If you have noticed such signs in the person with whom you speak, try to convey your thoughts more clearly to convince him of the truth of what was said. You do not want to be considered a deceiver? Like all other signs, scratching the nose does not necessarily give the person a brazen liar. But if your interlocutor scratched his nose several times during a conversation, it is worth looking for other signs of lying or silencing the truth.

Fun Exercise

I have already said that not all people are the same, that is, not all eye movements correspond to the model. But everyone makes some movement when they create a construction in their minds. The following exercise will help you learn how to determine when the other person comes up with something.

Step 1

Ask the interlocutor to present something, for example, Gioconda depicted in the painting by Leonardo da Vinci. Give him time to mentally see the picture and carefully watch the movements of the eyes.

Step 2

Ask the interviewee to present the same picture, but with some variations. For example, Mona Lisa, covered with a five-year-old child. Give him time again to mentally see the picture and watch his eyes. Your goal is to check whether it follows the system or uses some of its own movements in the design.

Step 3

Offer the interlocutor to submit something else and make sure that he performs the same movements all the time. (Just ask for a new picture, otherwise, the design will not work—he will just remember the previous exercise.)

Tone

You, probably, have already noticed: when a person is angry, his voice becomes thinner, shrill. Moreover, he begins to speak louder and louder than in the normal state. When we are sad, the opposite happens: the voice becomes muffled, throaty. The person speaks slower and quieter than usual.

When someone tells a lie and at the same time feels a sense of guilt, the same changes take place with his voice as during anger. His voice automatically becomes thinner and louder, and he speaks faster than usual. If a person is ashamed of himself, his voice sounds the same as if he were sad. He speaks slowly and subdued. If you notice any of these changes in the interlocutor's voice for no apparent reason, this may mean that he is lying to you.

Bill Clinton scratched his nose 26 times during the Lewinsky process.

As it turned out, not only psychologists and body language researchers followed Clinton's nose during this process, then the president's personal adviser on communication with the media forbade him to even touch his nose, because by scratching him he reduced the level of trust in himself to almost zero.

Speech

Those who lie are prone to making pauses in a speech where they should not be, for example in the middle of a sentence or before answering a question. In this way, people try to gain time. Liars may even moan something inarticulate, like "Uh-uh", while their brain is trying hard to come up with another lie. Sometimes a person even stutters with excitement.

It is common for a liar to repeat often, to say the same thing over and over again. Sometimes he begins to speak in long sentences—so long that it seems as if they have no end. And all this because a person is afraid that he will be interrupted. All these changes are a sign that not everything is in order in communication with this person and you should carefully look closely at him.

Changes in Word Usage

Liars often express themselves in words too. They begin to speak like they never said before, and such platitudes that the lie immediately becomes obvious. Sometimes even the liar himself realizes that he is all nonsense but simply cannot stop. Words seem to break out of the language.

Misty Remarks

Liars love to beat around the bush, to make vague hints, to wag the tongue, without denoting the essence of what they want to say. A liar can answer the following question:

"Well ... basically ... you can say that ... well, it could be ... maybe that ... probably ..."

Repeat and Repeat

Liars do not like to go into details. They would rather repeat the same lie over and over than explain something.

For a person who speaks the truth, it will not be difficult to supplement the information with new details or transfer it in a more compressed form. The memory is not something that we get out of the memory box, blow away the dust particles and put it back. The memory changes depending on the context in which it was addressed.

A person who speaks the truth can place accents in different ways, telling the same story several times. A liar always tells the same thing out of fear of being caught up in mismatches. However, he will not go into details. If you suspect a person is lying, ask them to clarify something. For example:

- I was alone all evening. I watched TV. Then he went to bed.

- What did you watch?

"I ... well ... this is ...

Pretentiousness

Liar is prone to using lush rhetoric, for which nothing stands. His speech is extremely abstract and even logically inconsistent. People try to create the illusion of clarity, when in fact nothing is clear. For example, the former mayor of New York, charged with tax evasion, said: "I did not commit a crime. I just did not follow the law," or Clinton on the question about the relationship with Miss Lewinsky:" It depends on how you look at it. "

Another classic example: "This question can be answered with both yes and no, depending on how it is formulated."

Do not forget that repressed actions (repressed gestures)—it is natural for a person. There are situations that trigger a burst of energy that we cannot find a way out of. In such situations, we are simply forced to snap our fingers, bite our nails or pull at a candle. There are periods in life when our energy level is above the norm. Look—what gets a teenager who was told to sit quietly?

Chapter 7 - Nonverbal Cues

The funny thing about communication is that most messages are non-verbal. The following are some of the common nonverbal cues.

Wearing a frown
When you spot someone with a frown on their face, it can only mean one thing: they're mad about something. Some people put a conscious effort into wearing a frown, but for others, it is more of an automatic response to unpleasant events. Someone with a constant habit of wearing a frown will appear distant

and aloof. For this reason, they may have difficulties establishing close relationships with other people. But there is a class of human beings who have not learned how to control the facial expression. They might seem to wear a frown when nothing is wrong with them. These people have a face that just looks tough.

Supporting your chin with your closed fist

In a scenario where people are rolling a conversation forward, and one of them puts their chin on their closed fist, it means that they don't agree with whatever is being said. The pose betrays their thought process, but they might not always speak up. It is upon the other party to notice the pose and bring it up. Then putting your chin on your fist might come across as rude to other people.

Covering your face with your hands

When someone covers their face with their hands, it might mean one of two things: they are exhausted or worried. The modern life is fraught with stressful living conditions. On every turn, there are things that could cause us significant emotional pain, and thus, it is easy to become overwhelmed with worry or grow tired. You might notice someone do that when they run into another task that requires their resources, or they may do it as a sign of increasing weariness.

Covering your mouth with your palm

If you are a twenty-year-old dude in college, and you messed with a girl, and she got pregnant. Think of how your mom would act when you disclosed that you were expecting a child. Maybe she would immediately cover her mouth with her palm, at a loss for words. This act shows that you are extremely shocked. It is what people normally do before they find the right words to express their shock.

Holding your lips in

Let's say you walk in on your spouse speaking on the phone and immediately she hangs up. Therefore, you try to understand why she hangs up. You ask her who she'd been talking to. But instead of disclosing, she holds her lips in. That's a clear sign that she doesn't want to continue this conversation. She's not okay with telling you whom she had been talking to. People hold their lips in when they feel uncomfortable talking about a certain topic.

Tilted head

Assuming you were in a social gathering, and as you were looking about, you spotted a woman to one corner, and then suddenly she tilted her head. That's the equivalent to her saying, "come hither!" A tilted head is always indicative of interest. And it usually means that the person has a high level of interest. If on top of a tilted head, they have their hands crossed against their pelvis it is an indication of nervousness. They are too scared that you will not reciprocate to their urge to talk to you.

Scratching the collarbone

This is the classic indicator of being overwhelmed. The average person has much too responsibilities to juggle, and yet the resources are limited. Think of the average lower-middle-class woman. Presumably, she must tend to her spouse, her children, her job, and show dedication in every instance. While she is in the office, you might see her scratching her collarbone as she processes all the burdens that she must bear for her life to sail smoothly.

Wide eyes

Our eyes are very communicative. It's all that one needs to see before they reach a conclusion. Wide eyes mean excitement. Think of a guy who just proposed to his fiancé, and she said yes. His anxious look is immediately replaced by his wide-eyed expression. But if the wide eyes are accompanied by a smile, it is an indication of nervousness. Eyes are probably the most expressive part of a human being. You can tell whether one is sad, happy, or angry, just by looking at their eyeballs.

A downward gaze

If you are trying to talk to someone, but they keep looking down, it can only mean one thing: they are disinterested. They would rather be elsewhere. But then again, a downward gaze might mean that the person is overwhelmed by your presence and that you intimidate them. If their body posture is generally pulled away from, you denote a far stronger disinterest.

Leaning in

When someone is leaning towards you, it means that they are interested in having you around. This is even truer when they open themselves up or put their hands on you. If their arms are wrapped around their midsection, they may be enjoying the moment, yes, but they are trying to hold back something. It is also important to check the direction that their feet points. Generally, our feet look towards the direction that we want to head. If their feet are pointing toward you, it means that they are interested in listening and connecting with you.

Interlocked fingers

Picture a woman whose husband is undergoing prostate surgery. She is standing on the hospital halls with her fingers interlocked. This is an indication that she's worried. The interlocking of hands over the chest region implies that the worry is even pronounced. It is usually accompanied by the act of moving about tensely.

Supporting your chin with your open hand

Picture a woman who's suspected her husband of cheating. So, she grabs his phone and goes through his messages, only to find a string of texts between him and a lover. The husband will, of course, come up with a story. But as his wife listens to that disjointed story, she may be resting her chin on her open hand. That pose is indicative of a loss of interest. When someone rests their chin on their hand, it usually means that they are tired of whatever is going on around them.

Head jutting forward

This position is indicative of aggression. Think back to your school going days. Think of how the boys acted (usually the bully versus the victim) when they were at the verge of exchanging blows. The one who has more pissed off will have his head jutting forward. The aggressive spirit of this position compounds when the person closes their hands into fists.

Arms at akimbo with your head pulled back

This is a bossy expression aimed at sizing up the other person. When someone thinks too highly of himself, he might put his arms at akimbo, and look every other person up and down, as though to size them up. This position comes across as being too condescending towards others.

Pointing a finger

People who have a tendency of pointing their fingers when making their point usually come across as being too passionate. When someone makes a statement and accompanies it with finger-pointing, their statement carries more prominence as opposed to if the same statement were made in a plain manner. Additionally, finger-pointing is indicative of an aggressive attitude.

Curling the body toward the belly

Think of a kid that spots his bully coming after him. The kid might instinctively curl towards his belly. He knows that he's about to face the music and that he's no match to his bully's power. So, curling toward his belly is an act of both submission and self-preservation.

People also act in this way when they are hit with heartbreaking news. Usually, the pain is so much, and they find themselves curling towards their belly.

The crossing of your arms

This is a clear indication that an individual is presently uncomfortable. It is also indicative of tension. Normally, when a person is in a situation that arouses their negative emotions, they might cross their arms to make themselves more comfortable. This position makes their negative emotions tolerable, and it acts as a restraint against doing something regrettable.

The crossing of arms can also indicate being mad about something. Think of a mother who cleans their baby, and then the baby runs outside and covers himself with dirt within a record five minutes. When the baby comes back into the house, its momma might cross her arms, wondering what punishment on earth is proportional with such naughty behavior.

Putting a hand on your chest

This position expresses sincerity. When someone puts a hand on their chest while making a statement, you are likely to believe them, as opposed to when the delivery had been any other way. When we see someone put their hand over their chest, we think that whatever they are saying is coming from their heart.

Thrusting the hip out

People take this position when defending themselves against criticism. Usually, they place a hand on their hip too. People who take on this position tend to have strong feelings about being right, and they hate it when they are held in a negative light. Thus, they must always fight back to disprove whatever criticisms raised toward them.

A backward flip of the hand

When someone flips their hand backward, they mean to deescalate a tense moment. Maybe they have said something that aroused strong feelings and the criticism started pouring in and so they are forced to flip their hand backward to fend off an attack. This usually happens when the person believes that they have not been understood.

Putting a hand about someone else

This is done when someone is extremely comfortable with someone else. It is a show of affection. It is not necessarily a show of romantic attraction, but the parties normally have a bond. When the mutual interest is just too much, you will see the parties holding their heads close together.

Jaw clenching

Have you ever been seated next to a person, and suddenly, you noticed their jaw twitch? You probably thought to yourself, "that's cool!" Except you didn't realize that that person is likely stressed. People tend to clench their jaws when they are in stressful situations. The stress could stem from an internal or external environment. Maybe it is their thoughts, or maybe it is something going on around them.

Exaggerated nodding

Everyone understands that nodding is a form of appreciating what the other party is saying. When we are speaking to someone, and we nod at regular intervals, it sends a positive message, encourages them to carry on. In a sense, it is a form of validation. But then you meet someone who nods every three seconds. It is not only distracting but a dead giveaway that they are insecure. They find themselves having to nod endlessly because they feel inadequate. If you notice that someone is nodding much too frequently, and are certain that it is their insecurities driving them into acting so, you might want to ask them to stop and explain their behavior. It is not one of your easiest conversations you will ever make, but it will be far impactful.

Raised eyebrows are a sign of discomfort

Human beings are in constant pursuit of comfort. All of their goals and aspirations are in one way or another tied to their grand pursuit of comfort. Thus, when they experience any form of discomfort, it is easily apparent. People raise their eyebrows when they are in uncomfortable situations. The feelings of discomfort might be triggered by one of the following: worry, fear, or surprise. If someone is expecting life-changing news, they might be preoccupied with negative thoughts, as they perhaps wonder what may happen to them if they fall short of their expectations. People usually experience fear when they run into threatening situations. And people get surprised when something contrary to their expectations takes place. The average person can express discomfort in various ways, but the commonest one is raising the eyebrows.

Erect body posture is a sign of confidence

If someone walks into a roomful of people with droopy shoulders and a weak posture, nobody will bother about the person, for he's shown in his body language that he holds no power. But if someone walks into the room with his shoulders held back and his posture upright, people will take notice, react positively toward him, for he clearly thinks highly of himself enough to have an upright posture. Even bullies are aware of their victims: they always go for those who stand as if their backs are broken, and they give those who stand upright a wide berth. Having poor posture may stem from low self-esteem, but it may also stem from sitting down for extended periods of time. If you are talking to someone and they assume a bent position, remind them to assume an erect position, and explain the benefit.

Copying other people indicates interest

Have you ever talked to a person and you came away with the feeling that they were copying your every act? For instance, if you crossed your feet, a few minutes later, they crossed their feet too. If you made a gesture, a short while later they also made it, and they had a tendency to rephrase your words. It may seem weird, but it is actually a good thing. It means that the other person is invested in you. Thus, they unconsciously reveal this attraction by mirroring both your words and actions.

Genuine smiles have crinkles at the corner of the eyes

The simple truth is that there's a lot of fakeness in today's world. You could run into someone who does not like you one bit and find him or her flashing you a smile – a fake one. It is in your best interest to determine whether a smile is genuine or not. A genuine smile is not just about the mouth but also about the eyes. The eyes appear as though they are emitting starlight. But most importantly, genuine smiles form crinkles around the eye corner. If you pay attention to a smile, you can really know whether it is fake or not. In addition, the capability of yours will no doubt save you a lot of heartbreak.

Nose touching

Honesty – there's a shortage of people who still obey this virtue. There are more liars than honest people in society. Not only can lies drive you into a painful situation, but the big lies can ruin your life. Thus, it is important to notice a liar when you are dealing with one. Psychologists say a liar has a tendency of touching their nose. Every human being has a moral compass. They know full well that telling lies is a betrayal of their morality. Some people might try to resist the nose-touching, but they eventually succumb to the unconscious touching of their nose. This is not to say that everyone who touches their nose while making a statement is a liar, but it gives you more opportunities to verify their authenticity. If they are touching their nose, and their story is disjointed, or there are much too contradictions; red flag!

Speaking quickly indicates tenseness

Someone with a tendency of speaking much too quickly is usually battling anxiety. They might even be struggling with low self-esteem. They speak fast because they don't consider themselves worthy of being listened too. Alternatively, maybe they imagine that whatever they have to say is of little importance and that people do not want to listen to you.

Close proximity indicates interest

If someone is doing all their best to come close to you, it only means that they are interested. Someone who was disinterested will try to pull back. When you're conversing with someone always check to see whether they are leaning in or pulling back. It tells you a lot about how they think about you.

Pocketing hands indicates anxiety

If you talk to someone and they are putting their hands in the pocket, it may mean that they lack the confidence to be themselves. They usually think that something is wrong with them. Their attempt to hide some of their body parts is indicative of their aversion to criticism. But then again, someone can pocket their hands when they are trying to hide something.

Staring eyes indicate intimidation

Have you ever been engrossed in a discussion with someone who wouldn't get their eyes off of you? He must have thought it was creepy, and rightly so. Someone who's staring at you non-stop might be trying to intimidate you. If you hold his gaze, you end up escalating the situation.

Tightened neck indicates stress

Someone who's having a hard time is likely to stiffen his neck. This move can also indicate annoyance, but for the most part, that person is struggling with a stressful moment. If you notice, someone is tightening his neck, you might want to ask what your contribution to his emotional instability is and remedy the situation.

Chapter 8 - Analyzing People In Dating And Love

Jim is a lady's man. He exudes a masculine charm and smooth way of communication that other men would kill for. He can attend a social gathering and have the woman of his choice.

On the other hand, Jane is every man's dream of a perfect woman. She is not the most pretty or well-dressed. But she exudes a feminine charm that draws men in. It is easy for her to get any date of her choice while others find it difficult to get the man they desire. As you can see from the above illustrations, Jim and Jane are living the life in terms of dating and courtship. They don't have to work hard to get the partner of their choice.

They may not be movie-star attractive, but they always seem to get lucky with their choices. So, what makes the difference between them and those who fail in dating?

You will get the answer to this question and learn how to analyze people in love and dating in this section. You will also learn how to properly use these attraction methods to attract who you want. I will also show you how to understand the physiological changes that take place when you encounter the opposite sex.

What Happens When You Meet the Opposite Sex?

According to Dr. Albert Scheflen, a renowned body language expert and the author of Body Language and the Social Order, there are different physiological changes that occur in the body when you come across the opposite sex.

For instance, a man walking toward a woman will strut out his chest in lieu of a slouched position, stand taller, and increase his muscle tone in preparation for the encounter.

On the other hand, a woman who's interested will push out her chest to increase her breast size, touch her hair, walk livelier, expose her wrists, and appear submissive. You can see the different physiological changes that took place as they walked toward each other.

Body language is undoubtedly one of the fundamental components of dating, and it reveals how ready, desperate, insecure, confident, sexy, attractive, or available we are. Some of these dating body language responses are learned while some are completely out of our control.

Those who are the most successful at dating have realized how to optimize their body language to create an aura of attraction.

Why Jim and Jane Are Successful

Research on animal courtship behaviors by zoologists reveals that female and male animals utilize a series of courtship behaviors, some of which are subtle while

104

others are obvious, with a large percentage of courtship behaviors done unconsciously.

For example, in many species of birds, the male puffs up his feathers and struts around the female while giving a vocal display to gain her attention. While the male performs his courtship behavior, the female shows little to no interest. This courtship behavior is similar to that performed by humans when dating begins.

Jim and Jane were able to perform a series of gestures that attracted the opposite sex. What's more? They were able to emphasize their sexual differences in order to look attractive to the opposite sex.

The secret of Jim's technique was to first stop women whose body language screams that they are available and then to send his own masculine dating gestures. Interested females return the appropriate feminine signal, giving him the go-ahead to continue to the next phase.

Jim knew what to look for, and women would describe him as sexy, passionate, masculine, and humorous. More so, they will describe him as someone who makes them feel feminine. On the other hand, men would describe Jim as arrogant, boring, and insincere due to their reaction to his success with the ladies.

Women like Jane are successful in the dating game because they are able to send the right signals to men and to analyze those like Jim, who are able to send back the signals.

In dating and love, women are more perceptive in analyzing dating signals while men are generally blind to these signals.

It's a Woman's World

Women call the shots in dating. Although if you ask a man who usually makes the first move during courtship, he would say that men do.

Studies show that women are the imitators of dating signals about 90 percent of the time. Any man who walks across to chat with a woman has done so after receiving positive signals from the woman. If, however, a man walks toward a woman without receiving a green light, there's a lower chance of success unless the man in question is Brad Pitt.

The Stages of Attraction

As mentioned earlier, women call the shots in dating or courtship. Therefore, a large part of this chapter will be focused on women and the attraction signals they give off. So, let's go through the five stages of attraction that we all pass through when we meet an attractive person.

Stage 1: Making Eye Contact

A lady will make eye contact with someone she fancies, and she will hold it long enough for the man to notice. Then she holds his gaze for a few seconds before she turns away. Now she has the man's attention.
The man will keep watching her to see if she repeats the eye contact. A woman needs to repeat the eye contact at least three times before the average man realizes the significance of the message—most men are not perceptive. This eye contact is repeated several times, and it's the beginning of attraction and flirtation.

Stage 2: Smiling

Once she has the man's attention, she delivers one or more half-smiles that are intended to give the prospective date a green light. Sadly, many men are not responsive to the half-smiles, leaving the woman to think that he has no interest in her.

Stage 3: Preening

This is the next stage after the half-smiles, and it involves heightening sexual differences. At this point, the woman sits up straight to push out her breasts and crosses the ankles or legs to show off her legs. If she is standing, she tilts her head sideways toward one shoulder and tilts her hips to one side.

She plays with her hair as if she is grooming herself for the man. She may straighten her clothes or jewelry or even lick her lips to make them more inviting.

The man will respond by standing up straight, expanding the chest, and pulling the stomach in. Lastly, they point their feet toward each other to show acceptance and willingness to proceed to the next stage.

Stage 4: Talk

The man, at this point, takes the active role by walking toward the woman in an attempt to make small talk. He will attempt to break the ice by using clichés, such as "You look familiar. Have I seen you somewhere?"

Step 5: Initiating Touch

After the initial small talk and well-used clichés to break the ice, the woman will look for an opportunity to initiate a light touch on the arms, either unintentionally or otherwise. Take note of these light touches. A touch on the hand is more intimate than a touch on the arm. Men can also initiate the light touch.

Though it feels less intrusive when it's first initiated by the woman. The light touch is then repeated to see if the person is happy with the first touch and to make them aware that the first touch was not accidental. She can also initiate a handshake to fast-track the connection.

To many, these five stages of attraction may seem minute or even incidental, but they are of great significance at the beginning of every relationship. This chapter will explore the likely signals sent by both men and women during the five stages of attraction.

Mirror, Mirror, Who's the Fairest in the Land?

In the famous Disney fairy tale, we saw the witch/queen asking the mirror to show her who's the fairest in the land. Well, most of us are familiar with how the story turned. If not, go brush up on Snow White and the Seven Dwarves.

When you are in the same emotional state as the other person, you tend to mirror or copy their posture. For instance, if the other person is in a sitting position with the legs crossed over another, you find yourself mirroring the person's posture as your connection grows deeper. This is why I refer to the mirroring signals as the sixth stage of attraction. Interestingly, you can mirror someone you are interested in even though the person is on the other side of the room. How awesome is that?

Common Male Dating Signals and Gestures

Men don't have as many dating signals or gestures in their repertoire. The male display generally revolves around shows of power, wealth, status, and masculinity. This is unlike women who have a range of gestures in their arsenal.

In this section, we will explore most of the male gestures you are likely to see during dating. A majority of these gestures are centered on the crotch region. Other gestures include standing tall, tucking the stomach, and pushing out the chest to boost his male presence.

He will smoothen his collar, straighten his tie, touch his watch or cuff links, brush an imaginary lint off his shoulders, and rearrange his coat or shirt.

The Male-Crotch Obsession

As mentioned earlier, a man's sexual display centers on placing emphasis on the crotch region. For instance, the thumbs-on-belt gesture is an aggressive display that highlights the crotch. When he's leaning against a wall or in a sitting position, he may also spread his leg to reveal his crotch region. He may also turn his body and foot toward you and use an intimate gaze to catch a woman's attention for a long time.

The crotch display is also observed in primates, where the male exerts dominance by sitting with their legs wide open to reveal the male organ. In New Guinea, natives use the penis sheath to assert their dominance and to exude sex appeal to the opposite sex.

On the other hand, some men in Western culture employ the use of tight-fitting pants or Speedo to accentuate the outline of their male organs.

The crotch adjust is also a common male form of sexual display that revolves around adjusting or handling the crotch. You will notice this gesture a lot when young males get together to show machoism.

Removal of Glasses

This gesture is common to both sexes. It's usually one of the signs that the person is lowering their barriers around you. It's more of an invitation that you are hitting the right buttons in the conversation. If instead, the glasses are held up between you then it is a strong signal that the person is not really buying what you are saying.

Puts Anything in the Mouth

Sometimes done by men, this gesture is frequently used by women to indicate interest.

Rhythmic Function

Swinging leg, toe tapping, fingers drumming, or leg bouncing on the tip of the toe are all movements that indicate the person is uninterested, impatient, nervous, or bored with what you have to say.

Closed Hands and Clenched Fists

The closed fists mean the other person has shut you out completely. It's a precursor to an angry or aggressive tone or outburst.

Chapter 9 - Interpreting Behavior Common Patterns And Analysis

Every tragic event makes us think of our own security. We would all like to know what misfortunes and fatalities await us in the future to be able to avoid them in time. But, fortunately, or unfortunately, this knowledge is beyond our reach. However, the years of experience of experts allowed identifying 6 basic characteristics that are inherent to potential criminals. Thanks to these signals, it is not difficult to realize if a person can represent a danger to society.

Change in Self-Perception

The psycho-emotional portrait of most criminals contains a common detail: a pronounced maximalist or minimalism in judgments, including self-perception. A person can exaggerate his own meaning to be considered a representation of the highest or, on the contrary, minimize their role in society.

For example, one of the attackers wrote in his personal diary: "I am God." This is a clearly expressed radical idea of his superiority over others. Undoubtedly, even without special education, it is possible to notice this type of deviations in human behavior. Especially if they are atypical for the person in question.

How it manifests:

Manic desire to express racial, gender, social and other types of superiority over others;

Unconscious underestimation of their importance to the rest of the world, relatives, and friends;

Categorical refusal to consider any other point of view that differs from their own.

Tendency Towards Dangerous Hobbies

It is worth saying that interest in cold or fire weapons is not a direct sign that a person is a potential criminal. Legal hunting, the collection of rare

knives or rifles, the love of computer shooting games is nothing more than a hobby. It is important to see and understand the line that separates a hobby from the manic tendency to deadly dangers.

But if a person admires psychopaths and criminals, expresses approval and respect for some radical ideas and goals, openly expresses extremism, it is a good reason to stay away.

Lack of Empathy for Another Person

As a general rule, a person with a tendency to self-destruction eradicates the feeling of compassion and empathy for others. In general, these people lie very well, are prone to violence and enjoy the torture and humiliation of other people.

The modern world is used to expressing their emotions and preferences in the most simple and accessible way: through social networks. Videos of category 18+ with scenes of cruelty and violence, aggressive appeals and slogans, membership in radical communities, are an important part of what should cause concern. Just looking at the content that interests a person, you can often understand what is more focused.

How it manifests itself:

Inability to sincere repentance for the works performed

The person does not express concern for the people around them

The person does not care about their own physical and emotional health

Great ability to manipulate other people to achieve their own goals.

Clear Mental Disorders

In this case, we are talking about inappropriate behavior that differs from established norms. It can be obvious aggressiveness or hatred towards other people and animals, mood swings for no reason, attempts to withdraw and abstract. In reality, the symptoms are many, but people who know their problems can hide them well. After all, in criminal practice, there are many cases of violent psychopaths that in the family environment were quite common people.

How it manifests:

Altered mental activity and behavioral reactions

Irrational aggression and sudden mood swings

Behavior that goes beyond the limits of existing moral and cultural norms

The person may feel inexplicably happy or unhappily unimportant about the events that occurred

Vague awareness of reality and inadequate perception of one's state

Problems in Contacting the Outside World

The desire to abstain from the outside world can arise for a number of reasons. It can be caused by a prolonged illness, a mental disorder, a long vacation or excessive use of modern technology.

The tendency to de-socialize in adolescents, school children or university students is often caused by bullying: psychological terror, persecution, beatings, and humiliation of one person by another. Children and adolescents, as a rule, try to hide this type of aggressive manifestations from others, considering it shameful. If you notice that your friend, son or relative is under pressure, then in no way should you turn a blind eye.

Depression

Here we are talking about real depression, not stress or a sad spell of bad luck. It is very important to distinguish these concepts, since depression is a mental disorder, while stress or a sad spell of bad luck is quite a natural phenomenon in the life of a person.

The experts distinguish several types of this disease, but all are united by these symptoms:

Apathy and lethargy, indifference, lack of emotions and desires

Sleep disorders, anxiety, fear, loss of concentration

Low self-esteem, a desire to hide from society

Thoughts about death, suicide, the afterlife, concentration on the negative moments of life

Alcohol abuse, refusal to eat or tendency to overeat, unwillingness to take care of one's appearance

What Is the Conclusion?

We all sometimes want to be alone, we all have bad mood days and even emotional overflows. So, before drawing conclusions, you must analyze all the components of the person's behavior, because many of our actions depend on the context of the situations in which we find ourselves.

And remember that most tragic events could have been avoided if someone had asked for help from another person on time.

Human Behavior Is Predictable By 93%

A study reveals certain patterns in our mobility, such as the fact that we always return to sites already visited. A team of researchers studied the mobility of thousands of people through the signals of their mobile phones. Thus, they have discovered that our displacements are always highly predictable, regardless of whether we move large or short distances. Knowing the patterns of human mobility, which are maintained in different social groups and environments, could serve to optimize urban development and public health policies.

What We Think About Our Future Determines Our Happiness

The electrical activity of the heart can already be simulated. Study shows that body language expresses our socioeconomic status. Religion is an effective regulator of human behavior. Some human behaviors have an evolutionary background. Human behavior is predictable by 93%, says a group of scientists.

The researcher came to this conclusion from an investigation in which the displacement patterns of anonymous users of mobile telephony were studied. Specifically, the journeys of a total of 50,000 people, chosen at random from a set of 10 million individuals, were analyzed over three months.

This study has revealed that, although it is generally believed that most of the actions that we take are unpredictable and random however humans follow regular patterns most of the time.

Spontaneous People Are Scarce

Spontaneous individuals are scarce among the population. Thus, although significant differences have been found in the travel patterns among the individuals studied, the movements of each one of them, separately, are equally predictable.

This predictability is, as has been said, of 93%, regardless of the distance that people travel when traveling: whether they move far from their homes or stay close to them, you can "guess" with the same exactitude they will find out in the next hour.

Another researcher points out that people usually assume that it is easier to predict people that travel very less as compared to people that travel over a thousand kilometers.

Back to The Known

However, this study has shown that, despite the heterogeneity of displacements, the movement of all individuals falls within what is expected.

Research has also shown another surprising aspect of population mobility: patterns of individual movements do not vary significantly depending on certain demographic categories, such as age, sex, population density or whether the location studied is rural or urban

In other previous research on mobility patterns, researchers studied the trajectories in real time of 100,000 anonymous mobile phone users. These users were also selected randomly, from a list of more than six million people.

In this case, the results were similar to those of the present investigation: the scientists verified that, in spite of the diversity of the travel history of each of the individuals analyzed, all followed reproducible mobility patterns.

For example, people, for more or fewer kilometers that travel, always have a strong tendency to return to locations they have visited previously.

What It Is For

As the scientists published, foreseeing the movements of people could serve as a management resource for mobile communications.

On the other hand, it would also be useful to make models for the expansion of epidemics, to carry out better urban planning or to design traffic more efficiently.

In general, being able to know scientifically how the population is going to move could have a positive impact on society, on public health policies and on urban development.

Be A Model of Behavior for A Teenager

In this section, we will talk about the importance of modeling and how to get your child to change through the imitation of other people or yourself. Keep in mind that modeling is one of the tools you can use to change your child's behavior.

Psychology has traditionally studied imitation. Human beings are social beings and nature has endowed us with an innate capacity to learn from others by repeating their behavior.

This is a fabulous way to maintain the culture at the level of society, but it is also a way to achieve a specific change in behavior in those who need it.

The basic idea of this technique is simple. Your child can change his behavior by watching other people do it and evaluating the consequences for them.

Imagine possible scenarios:

Discover the best educational tools to connect with your adolescent child. A course specially designed to improve communication at home and the motivation of your child.

Learn or increase a behavior before a model that gets rewards: think of a small child who sees another child get what he wants from adults when he cries or howls.

I remember the story of a friend who at 3 years old recognized being the class bully. He had a voice so unusually powerful for his age that when he cried, he frightened the rest of his classmates. Only for the teacher to shut up gave her any whim she had. Today, my friend admits having used this ability to make a profit. Sadly, other children of that same class learned their tricks from him, distributing not a few headaches among their families. In this example, the key is that my friend was publicly rewarded for his screams.

Decrease or eliminate a behavior in front of a punished model. As intelligent animals, we run away from situations in which we see others get into trouble. Imagine that your child contemplates how his classmates laugh at a boy with glasses. It is very likely that if one day he needs them he will resist using them or will ask you to wear contact lenses to avoid being discriminated against.

In both examples, there is a model that obtains some consequences of its social group for its behaviors. The people who surround this model learn from these consequences and try to repeat or avoid their behavior depending on whether they are rewarded or punished.

Characteristics of An Effective Model

As human beings, we have the ability to imitate models from our birth. This ability has been related to cooperative skills, socialization, and empathy.

Our brain contains a series of mirror neurons that are closely related to this ability. Thanks to them we can learn from the behaviors of other people just by observing them.

Interestingly, this ability to learn through imitation and mirror neurons has also been found in other animals such as primates and some birds. Therefore, it is not an exclusively human capacity.

Research on the type of behavior model for an adolescent has found some common characteristics:

They imitate people that are considered competent and are prestigious or have a social status.

Those people similar in age, sex and ethnicity will be considered as a model to imitate with greater probability. At this point, children and adolescents are an exception since they tend to imitate adult models as well.

They tend to emulate those models that obtain positive consequences for their observed behaviors. My friend was imitated by his companions because shouting invariably won a prize.

Television as A Role Model for A Teenager

One of the curiosities that have been found in research on imitation is that modeling can occur from a person present or be symbolic, without there being a real reference.

That is to say, learning and imitating behavior can be produced by watching a video or listening to a sound recording. This is a very common phenomenon that happens continuously in our society, also in the adult world.

We can even affirm that television is the main behavioral model of our society. Films and advertising are two great schools of conduct for us and day by day they create a trend in our culture.

Television can become a role model for a teenager. Just think about how the European Union faced the power of the big tobacco companies to ban tobacco advertising in the press, radio, and Internet starting in 2005.

Parents in the Cloud Courses

Sign up for the best courses to educate your adolescent child. You will discover the most effective techniques to achieve an improvement in communication and motivation in your home.

It is difficult to know which models your child will choose to imitate during his adolescence. But you can try to become a model. For this, we propose the following strategies that as a parent you can use to achieve it.

Use more than one model whenever possible: studies show that it is much more effective if the behavior occurs in several people. Imagine that you educate your son so that he does not smoke and you are a model for him because you do not do it. Imitation will be much more effective if neither your partner nor your school teachers smoke. This is effective because it will make more credible for your child what you observe. That is, the greater the number of models that comply with the behavior, the greater the probability of imitation.

Pose behaviors to imitate that do not exceed the capacity of your child: it seems obvious but think if sometimes you have expected your child to imitate your behaviors that he may not understand or may not be able to repeat. Ideally, the behavior model for an adolescent of this type of complex behavior begins with simple acts and gradually becomes more complicated. A typical example of this point would be that your child is able to make the purchase independently. Although now you do not see it, this behavior includes many repertoires of different abilities that you can divide and go modeling little by little. Locate the products, calculate the price, interact with the supermarket workers and so on.

Perception of the consequences of the behaviors: it will be much more effective for your child to see how a friend of his who has disrespected a teacher gets his punishment. If this happens, you can anticipate the consequences of repeating those types of behaviors and it will be easier for you not to repeat them.

Reward the successes: if your son manages to replicate the behavior you want him to imitate, reward him for it. It will be the best way to accelerate the imitation process and thus you will understand directly that you are on the right track and that you have your approval.

Chapter 10 - Possible Exceptions In Analyzing People

The concept of truth is relative. What is true to you might not be the universal truth. The universal truth, in some cases, might not always be the truth. The truth will depend on the context of the conversation. Let's use this example to illustrate this point:

"Your football team plays well and creates many chances, but you lose the game on penalties. This is a game that, by the chances created and the style of play, you should have won."

Did you play well? The answer depends on the perspective. You lost the game, so it is fair for an outsider to believe you did not play well. However, someone intimate with the game who watched it knows this is not true. They know you played well, outdid yourselves, but somehow, lost the game on penalties. Anyone who understands the game knows that when it comes to penalties, anything is possible.

So the truth is that you did play well. However, you did not win. It is not easy to reconcile these two realities. This is why you will often find coaches lamenting after a game that the best team lost.

The fact that the truth can be relative is one of the biggest risks to the concept of the truth. People can twist the truth to suit their context. In psychology, it is important that you learn how to identify irrational thoughts, which manifest into cognitive distortions. These distortions affect your mental strength. The longer they manifest, the weaker your mental resolve becomes.

When analyzing people, you have to be aware of the fact that everything you do is about communication, and communication works both ways. You can only receive as much as you are willing to give. There are some exceptions that you should remember because, if you don't, you might easily lose the plot and give in to your personal bias, which eventually affects the way you read people.

Personalizing the Situation. In your interactions, it is healthy to assume that the world does not revolve around you because, to be honest, it doesn't. However, this assumption and awareness of its effect are two different things. When you personalize issues, you affect the way your brain digests the message. This, in turn, affects the message you send back, and before you know it, the whole communication paradigm is distorted.

Catastrophizing. If you think about something for so long, it might just happen. This is mainly about negative thoughts and sentiments. People never really understand the risks involved when they empower the negativity in their minds like this. You have to try to keep an open mind about everything. Do not pass judgment on someone before you meet them. If you do, you become anxious about the meeting, and when you see them, your focus might be distracted by something they say or do. An innocent mistake might have you thinking, "I knew you'd do that anyway," robbing you the chance to communicate with someone openly and honestly.

Generalizations. The problem with generalizations is that they limit your choices and your effort. Once you generalize about someone, it is difficult to see them differently. In your mind, they can only be as good as the cluster you put them in. If they try something different, you wonder why they thought about that in the first place. Generalizations prevent you from establishing authentic connection and communication with people.

Mind Reading. It is ironic that, as we try to learn how to read and analyze people, mind reading is one of the things that might make this impossible. How is this so? You are trying to read someone based on what they present before you. Your analysis should be built on tangible evidence, what they say, how they say it, how they proved it, and so forth.

What you think is going through their mind is not tangible. You have no proof that they think you are an idiot. You have no proof that they feel you are not the right person for the job unless they say it. Mind reading will often make you conclude someone without allowing them a fair chance to represent themselves. The result is that you don't understand each other at all.

These errors are more common in communication than you know. What you need to do is challenge the thoughts when they come across instead of feeding them. An evidence-based approach is the best way to deal with these exceptions. If you don't have evidence to prove that something happened, your thoughts about it happening are not true. Scrap it all together and allow the other person to proceed.

Changing your thoughts is just as difficult as learning about yourself. It might be difficult at first, but the more you practice and learn what to do, it becomes easier.

Chapter 11 - Speed Reading

Speed reading is a technique to increase reading without compromising understanding and retention of information. There are several different methods of speed reading, but they all aim to read clearly, but faster.

For those who work as a freelancer, especially the producers of web content, digital marketing, etc., reading is a prime activity. And speed reading lets you take even more of the time you have available for this activity. It is through reading that you deepen your knowledge to argue more strongly and keep your repertoire of subjects relevant and up to date. Unfortunately, it is not always possible to devote the time needed to complete reading an article or a book. In this situation, speed reading helps you extract the most important information in less time.

What Is Speed Reading?

Speed reading is a technique that seeks to increase the reading speed without compromising understanding and retention of information. There are several different speed-reading methods for both books and online texts and they all aim to read clearly as well as faster.

Check out this step by step guide and learn how to enhance your speed-reading skills!

1. Train your eyes to make bigger jumps

Do you know how the movement of your eyes works while reading? Basically, it's a jumping move. Your eyes pin one point on the line and then jump to the next. The higher this leap, the more proficient is your reading. Beginner readers, like children, skip only one word at a time and therefore take longer to finish each line. Therefore, the first step of speed reading is to train the eye movement so that it is wider.

2. Go straight ahead

The second step is to control that anxiety, that sense of obligation to understand 100% of the text. We are going to take this up further, but know that 80% understanding is an excellent goal.

In other words, you do not have to return to the beginning of the page every time you do not understand a line. After all, re-reading can take a long time - and that is precisely what we are trying to avoid.

In addition, you can fully understand the general idea of a text, even though some excerpts are more confusing. Then, after finishing the text, resume only the parts where you have doubts. But if you stop and go back constantly, you will never finish reading.

Another important tip is to not interrupt the reading to check the dictionary. If you are very curious about the meaning of a word, write it down to check later. However, do not abandon the text to browse the dictionary because when you return, it will take you even longer to resume reading.

In the meantime, try to understand the term by context - you may not absorb the exact meaning of the word, but it will be enough to understand the message the author wanted to convey.

3. Stop speaking the words

The third step is to eliminate a negative practice that is a habit of many people: to pronounce the words as they read, either loudly or mentally.

This habit prevents the development of speed reading because it means that you will literally read word for word.

The speed slows down and as incredible as it may seem, the capacity for understanding as well. Because your brain will be busy with pronunciation, you will not be able to concentrate on interpreting what you are reading. The result is that you will have to reread the same stretch several times.

If you are too accustomed to pronounce as you read, losing this habit can be a difficult and time-consuming process. An interesting tip is to put a pencil in your mouth as you read. With a little practice, you will lose this "craze" and see how it improves your reading time.

4. Use skimming technique

The fourth step is "skimming." This is a well-known technique for Instrumental English, but it is also useful for speed reading in any language.

Skimming consists basically of looking quickly through a text in order to extract basic information - index, title, author, date of publication, main subject, subtopics developed, graphics and images.

This technique is useful for you to quickly evaluate any text and then set whether to devote more time to a full reading.

If you are researching on a specific subject, for example, skimming will allow you to identify whether a particular article or book has relevant information about the subject. In addition, you will find the excerpts that interest you more easily.

5. Use the scanning technique

The fifth step, "scanning," is another technique used in English Instrumental. It consists basically of looking at the text to identify keywords, which in this case are relevant terms, related to the information you want to extract from that content.

Suppose you are reading a twenty-page article on People Management, but the subject that really matters to you is Productivity. In that case, you do not have to read all twenty pages - which will certainly tell you about various other issues that are not important to you right now.

Instead, just look through the article for terms directly related to productivity, such as "time," "organization," "concentration," and so on. When you find one of these terms, you just need to read that passage. Thus, you quickly get information that is of interest to you and "skip" the rest.

6. Monitor your performance

Once you incorporate what you have learned in the first five steps, the evolution of your speed reading will depend on practice. But to see if it's working, you need to keep track of your progress.

So, the sixth step is picking up a timer and monitoring how many words you read per minute. As a reference, keep in mind that a typical reader reads, on average, 150 words per minute. Meanwhile, a good speed-reading practitioner can read up to 800 words per minute.

But do not just monitor speed. Take into account, also, the use of reading, that is, how much you can understand the text without having to return to it a second time. Your goal should be an average of 80% utilization.

Remember that there is no point in speeding up reading, and thereby lessening the understanding of what has been read, as the re-reading also represents a waste of time.

7. Train Your Focusing Ability

Now that we've covered the best strategies for speed reading itself, let's take a few tips that will enhance your reading experience as a whole and as a result, help you absorb more information in less time.

The ability to stay focused while reading is critical to being productive and not wasting time. The deeper you "plunge" into the text, the better you understand what the author wrote.

What happens, then, if you go to every two paragraphs to check the notifications on your cell phone? The experience will be interrupted and continually resumed, which diminishes your ability to comprehend and thus takes you to take more time to understand what is read.

In this way, you waste twice as much time: the extra time it takes to understand what you read and the precious minutes wasted with distractions (Smartphone, computer, social networks, etc.).

If you often suffer from it, the key is to turn productivity into a habit. To do so, when you read, keep the distractions away. This means not leaving the phone nearby, not keeping the computer by your side and, if possible, turning off the internet or at least placing your devices in airplane mode.

This time is for you to dedicate to the text and nothing else! The more you can focus on reading, the better your ability to practice speed reading.

8. Find a quiet place to do your reading

The place you choose to do your readings also greatly influences the speed and dynamism of the activity - something very connected to the danger represented by the distractions, as we just mentioned.

Noise from traffic, from work, from an establishment (such as a bar, for example) and even from music can disturb your ability to concentrate, making you frequently "quit" reading. Also, if you are reading in an environment with other people, you will also be directly interrupted if they speak to you, even if it is a quick dialogue.

Besides being silent, it is also important that the chosen corner for reading is comfortable. When you are comfortable reading, it is much easier to indulge in the text and devote your full attention to it. And if you have a special space where you like to read, another advantage is that this will make it easier to establish reading as an integral part of your routine.

9. Do not insist when you are tired

You may have heard that it is not very productive for a student to spend the night studying for a test that will be given the next day. At that point, the desperation of a few extra hours of study is no longer as important as the rest, which will allow more focus and better memory for the student during the test.

The same principle can be applied to speed reading. When we are tired, regardless of whether the exhaustion reaches our site and/or head, our ability to concentrate decreases dramatically. You will find yourself having to read and reread the same passage several times, and of course, it takes much longer to read each line.

And the worst part is that the next day you can pick up the text and realize you cannot remember much of anything you read the night before. This is because a tired brain also decreases its ability to retain information.

So, an important point of speed reading is to know the time to stop.

10. Read whenever you can

What the reader does not like to sit in their favorite armchair and deliver hours and hours to a book or even a relevant and high-quality text? However, as you well know, this is not always (or rather, almost never!) possible.

Does this mean, then, that you are bound to a routine? Of course not! It turns out you do not have to self-punch yourself for not being able to devote several hours of each day to reading.

Start enjoying every free minute, especially with regards to idle time spent in queues, waiting rooms, or on public transportation, for example. And how about going a little early to bed, every night, and reading before bed?

A block of fifteen or twenty minutes in which you would do nothing when dedicated to reading becomes time well spent. With this, you advance much faster in your readings, although you cannot read much each day. Another advantage is that this will help you build the daily habit of reading - and, who knows, it will even encourage you to separate a few hours of your day into the activity.

Do you already practice speed reading? What is your speed and reading achievement? If you have not yet reached the goals proposed here, do not worry. Reading is a habit you cannot be afraid to develop, and the benefits are gigantic.

Keep in mind, however, that the tendency is to improve your vocabulary with constant reading. And with a complete vocabulary, you will have more and more facility to read and understand longer texts.

Essential Tips You Should Know About Speed Reading

Learn how to read more quickly by ensuring that all the content you learn is not lost in your mind after a few days.

Answer quickly! Do you read fast or slow? Have you ever tried to calculate your reading speed? By chance, have you heard of dynamic reading?

If not, you should. Well, if you love reading or even depending on it for studies, this advanced reading mode could help you a lot!

Dynamic reading is a faster type of reading which makes you read a lot in a short time. You may be thinking: reading fast is easy, but you cannot memorize it that way. Therefore, dynamic reading ensures this without impairing its ability to absorb content.

We've prepared some essential tips for you to start increasing your reading speed.

Understand: There are different types of reading speed. There are some reading differences that you may not know about and it is important to know. As we said, a more agile and concentrated reading reduces the time needed for learning. Therefore, it optimizes productivity and ensures that all content learned is not lost in your mind after a few days.

And this is essential for students, contestants, or even law and medical market professionals who need to read constantly. But this is not restricted to a group of people. Dynamic reading can help someone who already has a habit of reading to make you a reader with an even greater repertoire.

It must be understood that dynamic reading has two fundamental factors: content speed and retention. In short, reading too slowly can hinder the progress of any reading, or studies. Just like reading too fast and not understanding the subject is not good either.

Therefore, it is essential to find a balance by reading at a fast speed that does not detract from the retention of information.

Valuable tips for anyone who wants to start dynamic reading!

- Start slowly. Read every 15 minutes free!

- Subtract only minutes from your daily activities to read.

- Walk around with a book in hand and use short spaces of time to read.

- Read for 20 minutes while waiting for dinner to be ready in the oven.

- Read while waiting for the bus to work and if possible, even within driving.

With time and practice, dynamic reading will already be in your effortlessly!

Take A Test to Know How Long Your Reading Speed Is! The measure used to calculate the reading speed is the number of words read per minute (PPM). Usually, an average person with a reading habit reads about 250 words per minute. To know how to calculate, follow these steps:

Count the number of words in the first 3 lines of the same text. If you are reading in Word, it shows you how many words in the text.

Divide the total number of words from the first 3 lines by 3. The result will be the average number of words per line.

Multiply the average number of words per line by the number of lines you read in a minute. The end result will be your PPM index.

Let's see in practice:

Let's say that the first three lines of a text have 29 words. Therefore, the average number of words per line would be 9.6 (29/3 = 9.6).

Now imagine that you have read 30 lines of that same text in 1 minute. In this case, its result would be 288 PPM (30 × 9.6).

That is, a result of an ordinary reader, but still slightly above the average of 250 PPM.

Now that you have the result in hand, start with the first tip. Start by reading slowly for a few minutes. When you feel comfortable, improve your reading speed. Therefore, determine a goal for yourself and try to fulfill it. You must have a goal before anything else. Redo the calculations. Do not worry if you initially get below average. It is totally understandable and normal. In fact, if you are well above average, you probably have not performed the exercise correctly. And there is only one way of knowing if you have unconsciously not sabotaged yourself: try to explain the content of what has been read to someone. This is the best way to prove that your content retention was good.

Increase your reading speed. The best way to read faster is to practice reading every day. The more you read, the faster it gets. And you can start doing that already.

Chapter 12 - Persuasion Vs. Manipulation

Persuasion

When you hear the word persuasion, what comes to your mind? Maybe the advertising jingles of a product urging you to buy a pizza from them, or maybe political campaign slogans trying to convince you to vote for a particular candidate, or maybe a pushy salesman trying to sell you a car. You are absolutely right if you think those are acts of persuasion! Politicians, news, mass media, legal proceedings and advertising can persuade you and influence your decision making. Most people like to think that they are immune to such influences. But then most of us own Nike sneakers, Ray Ban sunglasses or of course the new I-Phone. So advertising must have played a role in influencing your decision. Persuasion is constitutional within human communication and social interaction. When communicating, wittingly or unwittingly, people are always supporting and/or promoting certain ideas and behaviors over others. Therefore, persuasion is intrinsic to social interaction and not a matter of choice.

Persuasion incorporates symbols, verbal and non verbal, to change attitudes. For example, images like Nike Swoosh or Adidas Three Stripes; words like freedom and justice; non verbal signs like Holy Cross or Star of David.

Persuasion involves a conscious and thoughtful attempt to influence another person. The persuader is always aware of the potential susceptibility of the person to accept change.

Persuasion is a voluntary act of changing our own attitude or behavior.

Persuasion is completely driven by the science of communication and requires a relay of verbal or non verbal message to the persuaded.

Persuasion of the self is at the heart of the art of Persuasion. People must always be free to decide if and how they want to change their attitude and behavior.

In 1980, Gerald Miller, suggested that communications can exert different persuasive effects, namely:

Shaping - For example, the Nike ad campaign featuring Michael Jordan connecting the Nike Swoosh with the idea of superhuman athleticism.

Reinforcing - For example, health experts make public statements to bolster the people's continuing resolve to abstain from excessive drinking.

Changing – For example, the civil rights campaigns increased dialogue between Blacks and Whites and brought about radical changes in the

Perhaps the foremost rule of good persuasion is stating suggestions using value-free verbiage. Persuasive is a positive act made in an attempt to alter people's opinion. For example, if you were visiting abroad and walked into a restaurant. You are very hungry but confused as to what you should order. As you are looking through the menu you come across a section labelled "Most Popular Dishes" or "Specialties", you are very likely to order a dish from that section.

Ethos (Character)

Aristotle suggested three major contributing factors to Ethos: "good moral character (arête); goodwill (eunoia); and good sense (phronesis)". The persuader must be able to build credibility and rapport with their audience. The word "Ethics" is in fact derived from "Ethos". Ethos, the ethical appeal, refers to the author's character and credibility as perceived by the audience. For instance, if you were sick and your doctor recommended treatment A and your close friend who has no medical background recommended treatment B, you will definitely choose treatment A since it was recommended by someone you think has credibility in that field. But odds are you are more likely to take a recommendation on new movies from your friend than your doctor.

Pathos (Emotion/Empathy)

Widely used colloquial term such as apathy, sympathy, pathetic and of course empathy is derived from

"Pathos". Pathos can be defined as an act of using shared stories and experiences to invoke emotions in the audience. In Greek language, Pathos means suffering and experience. This method can be used to draw pity or incite anger in the audience, to prompt them into action.

Aristotle suggested these mutually exclusive positive and negative emotions, that can be used by the persuader to build empathy with their audience: "Anger and Calmness; Envy and Emulation; Enmity and Friendship; Fear and Confidence; Kindness and Unkindness; Pity and Indignation; Shame and Shamelessness".

The powerful tool of Pathos, allows the persuader to stir desired emotions in the audience, by creating a bond and building empathy. The power of Empathy must not be undermined as human emotions always trump reasoning. Look at our history, the most influential political leaders were able to win their arguments by emotionally and empathetically persuading their audiences. For example, Martin Luther King, Jr's "I have a dream" speech, was able to invoke empathy for Black community in the White community and had a revolutionary effect in shaping the modern America.

The art of building Empathy

By building empathy, audience is more receptive to their persuader's message. To be able to successfully persuade your audience, you must be able to understand the pre-disposed emotions of your audience. Take your audience's state of mind in consideration and assess why they feel that way and to whom those emotions are directed at. Your ability to build empathy and emotional connection with your audience, in turn, builds your Ethos (character and credibility) with the audience.

Here are few ways to help you build empathy with your audience:

We are all human! - If you can easily blend in with your audience and make them see you as a part of their own "community", people will inevitably connect with you emotionally.

Be authentic – Nobody wants to be manipulated. If your audience suspects that you have ulterior motives and are not genuinely "one of them", you will lose all your credibility instantly.

Structure your statements to resonate with the audience. Every topic has multiple aspects and underlying perspectives to it. The key is to find what would work with your audience. For example, there might be speakers headlining to talk about preservation of wildlife. One might state "You can make a difference - Wildlife needs our help!" and other might state "Symposium on wildlife preservation". I know which speaker I will be listening to.

Narrate a story – Human psyche is hardwired to exhibit emotional responses to stories. Stories tend to be more memorable and inspire action. Personal stories have huge impact in building empathy but you could also share stories of someone you know or even fables. The act of story telling will give an impression to your audience that you have an understanding of the underlying emotion and your take on it.

Metaphorical speech – Similar to story telling, metaphors tend to be more memorable and make your speech intriguing. In words of Aristotle, metaphors give charm, clearness and distinction to your speech like no other. For example, MLK's use of banking metaphor in his "I have a dream speech", was met with thunderous applause. MLK said "Instead of honoring this sacred obligation, America has given the Negro people a bad check, a check which has come back marked "insufficient funds." But we refuse to believe that the bank of justice is bankrupt. We refuse to believe that there are insufficient funds in the great vaults of opportunity of this nation. And so, we've come to cash this check, a check that will give us upon demand the riches of freedom and the security of justice."

Use visual aids – Remember "A picture is worth a thousand words"! Using powerful images will incite emotions and help build empathy with the audience. For example, recently a picture of a Syrian boy bruised and helpless went viral, because it created a wave of empathy for the survivors of the ongoing Syrian war.

Delivery of speech – It goes without saying that your tone and volume of the speech must befit your audience.

Power of words – The English language has a bountiful of synonyms for everyday terms, providing a spectrum of intensity for the same emotion. For example, pain and agony; hungry and starving or sad and devastated. Have a thesaurus handy and use appropriate words.

Logos (Logic/Reasoning)

The word "logic" is, you guessed it, derived from Logos. In Greek language, Logos literally means "word". Logos refers to the act of appealing to the mind of your audience, using logic or reason. The effective persuader recognizes that using Logos alone, without Pathos and Ethos, poses them with a risk of losing their audience. With this type of persuasion, only facts and statistics can be employed in altering the attitude and behavior of the audience. There is no room for lies and deception. The appeal to reason is a measured and careful representation of facts and information in a logical way. The theory of logic can be categorized into two: Deductive reasoning and Inductive reasoning.

Deductive Reasoning – It's based on the assumption that if the premise is true, the conclusion would be true as well. For example, if the assumption is children love ice cream and you are presented with premise that Jack is a child. You can safely conclude that Jack loves ice cream.

Inductive Reasoning – As expected, Inductive reasoning is reverse engineering the premise from conclusion. Therefore, even if the premise is true, the conclusion may be false. For example, if the premise is 25% of American athletes like to read, the conclusion that 25% of American population likes to read may or may not be true.

Manipulation

Psychological Manipulation can be defined as a way to influence people's emotions, attitudes or behaviors which is neither rational persuasion nor coercion. The term manipulation is inherently thought of as negative and involving an element of moral deprecation. Human beings are inherently gregarious which makes them influence one another all the time. Consider, the influence your older sibling had on you growing up. That is a classic example of "healthy social influence" and must not be confused with the dark act of manipulation. In Psychological Manipulation, the goal of the manipulator is always to influence their victim into fulfilling their own desires.

People often confuse "manipulation" with "influencing" but they are poles apart in practice. Starting with the intent and motive of the person; an influencer is often looking for your best interest and approaches you with advice on how to make a decision better; but a manipulator has the mindset of how can I control your thoughts and emotions to get a better decision from you for myself. Thus, understanding the motive behind any such behavior plays a pivotal role in deciding whether it is a situation of "influencing", "manipulation" or even Covert Emotional Manipulation.

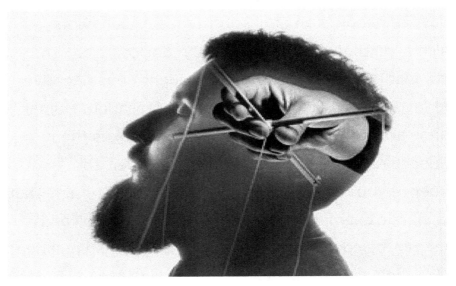

Covert Emotional Manipulation

The most widespread form of manifestation of Dark Psychology in today's world, which after reading this book you might agree with is Covert Emotional Manipulation (CEM). Now you are probably thinking is that different from Emotional Manipulation and if so, how. The answer is Emotional Manipulation occurs within the realms of your consciousness so you are aware that someone is trying to appeal to a more generous side of you to get what they want. Think about the time when your parents wanted you to visit them for the summer but you had a different probably more exciting summer plans with your friends or a special someone and your parents insisted you visit them instead or take some extra time off to make the visit. You tried to convince them that you would visit for Thanksgiving and your calendar is booked solid and they might have retorted with statements like "we are old and we wouldn't be around for so long, you need to make us your priority" or "we haven't seen you in forever and we miss you, come over to visit your loving parents". During this conversation you are completely aware that your parents are attempting to change how you feel about your summer plans in their favor. This is a classic and harmless case of Emotional Manipulation. On the other hand, Covert Emotional Manipulation is carried out by individuals who are trying to gain influence over your thought process and feelings, with the means of subtle underhanded tactics that go undetected by the person being manipulated.

By definition Covert Emotional Manipulation goes undetected and leaves you acting like a pawn in the hands of the manipulator, which makes this a manifestation of Dark Psychology. The dictionary definition of the word covert is "not openly shown or engaged in", therefore, it presents a stark difference from all other Emotional Manipulation techniques. The victims of Covert Emotional Manipulation are unable to understand the intent or motivation of the manipulator and the way they are being manipulation and even just the fact that they are being manipulated. Think of Covert Emotional Manipulation as a bomber with impeccable stealth, one that can tip toe in your subconscious without being detected, leaving you with no defense what so ever. Our emotions primarily dictate all other aspects of our personality and thus they also dictate our reality. Someone attempting to manipulate your emotions is equivalent to them cutting open your jugular vein making you lose control over yourself and your reality.

In this book, we have also covered some prominent and dark types of Manipulation, namely, Machiavellianism and Brainwashing in detail. But the are many more types of Psychological Manipulation in our society. Let's have a brief look at some of the more frequently observed forms of dark manipulation.

Gaslighting

The tactic used by manipulators aimed at making their victim doubt their own thoughts and feelings is called

Gaslighting. This term is often used by mental health professionals to describe the manipulative behavior to convince the victim into thinking their thoughts and feelings are off base and not in alignment with the situation at hand.

Passive-Aggressive behavior

Manipulators can adopt this duplicitous behavior to criticize, change or intervene the behavior of their victim without making direct requests or aggressive gestures. Some of these traits include: sulking or giving the silent treatment, portraying themselves as a victim or intentionally cryptic speech.

Withholding information

There is no such thing as a white lie but manipulators often provide selective information to their victim, so as to guide them into their web of deception.

Isolation

Dark manipulator is always aiming to gain control and authority on their victim. In order to succeed they will create an increasingly isolated environment for their victim and prevent them from contacting their friends and family.

The many differences between Persuasion and Manipulation

Motive/Intent

As we have established people with active dark psychological traits including manipulators, aim to establish control and authority on their prey and exploit their victims to serve their own interests. On the other hand, persuaders are concerned about the well being of their audience and attempt to convince them to change their attitude or behavior in a free environment.

Method of Delivery

Manipulators create an inviting environment for their victim, who is often an unwilling prey and primed emotionally and psychologically to act in ways that benefit their predators and threatens their own health or well-being. Whereas, persuaders only hope that their audience will respond to their influence and the suggestions. Ultimately the individual is free to decide whether or not they want to accept the suggestions made by their persuader and alter their thoughts, feelings and/or behaviors.

Impact on the social interaction

Dark manipulators will always aim to isolate their prey from the rest of the world and prevent any contact from their loved ones. The victim of dark manipulation like brainwashing, develop extreme views and may commit heinous acts of antisocial behavior. Unlike manipulation, acts of persuasion are never lethal for the audience and the society. It could be as harmless as your brother's admiration for Nike shoes leading you to buy a pair of your own or the ads from McDonalds inviting you to enjoy a quick meal with your family.

Final outcome

Persuasion usually result in one of these three possible scenarios: Benefit to both the persuaded and the persuader, commonly known as a win-win situation; Benefit only to the persuaded; Benefit to the persuaded and a third party. However, dark manipulation always has a singular benefactor that is the manipulator. The manipulated individual is at grave disadvantage and will act against their own self interest.

To drive this difference home, let's consider this example. Brian is on a budget and walks in the store looking to buy a new Smart TV. He is greeted by Adam, who then proceeds to show him all the Smart TVs available in the store. Adam explains to Brian all the unique features of different models and says "So and so Samsung model is little over your budget but it is the hottest product on the market with the best audio and video quality and is worth going over your budget".

Now, If Adam truly believes in his recommended TV model and has the best interest at heart for his customer. That's definitely act of Persuasion. On the other hand, if it so happens that Adam's recommended is not really worth its high price but that sale would make him extra commission, so he convinced Brian into buying a bad product at high cost. That's manipulation! Now that you have an understanding of Dark Psychology of manipulation, I offer you few scenarios in which dark manipulation can take place so you are armed to be able to detect it and protect yourself.

Disengage. If someone is trying to get on your good side and then ask for an overwhelming favor, simply decline politely and move on with the conversation.

Don't second guess yourself. Manipulators will try to convince you that your thoughts and behaviors are off base. Take a moment and assess whether the suggestion made by the person will benefit them or yourself and act accordingly.

Call them out. If you have successfully spotted the manipulation, don't be afraid to address the situation in a logical, respectful manner. Use of accusatory tone with a friend will just ruin your friendship so decide the sentence based on the crime.

Don't let them digress when you have spotted the manipulation. The manipulator and especially covert emotionally manipulator will not be prepared to get caught and will try to muddle the situation so as to minimize the harm.

If you are being probed to give out personal information, don't play in the hands of the manipulator. The manipulator is attempting to baseline your thought process and behavior to evaluate your strengths and pounce on your weaknesses.

Ask for details. Remember manipulators seek to withhold information from you so as to paint their own version of reality for you. If you feel you are being presented with a partial view of the situation, grill them for more information and make sound decisions.

Beware of exaggeration. Some manipulators can adopt an opposite approach and bombard you with additional and often vague details about the situation, in order to confuse you or even mentally exhaust you to cave in and accept the manipulation.

Verify the facts. Lying and deception come naturally to the manipulator. They will often manipulate facts or present false information to pressure you into making a hasty decision. Do not fall for the lies and "Google" your way to safety!

Scrutinize the bureaucracy. Certain manipulators may try to intimidate you with paperwork, procedures and laws to exert their power and authority. Don't undermine yourself and read through the paperwork and research the procedure and laws. Make well informed decisions

Don't be intimidated by their aggressive behavior. Some manipulators will play out front and center. They will raise their voice or display negative emotions with strong body language, to make you submit to their coercion. Stay strong and firm!

Take your time. I cannot emphasize this enough. If someone is rushing you into making a decision, by creating false deadlines or conveying a sense of urgency for your benefit, be sure to take control, step back and make a well informed decision.

See through those negative remarks and criticism. Skilled dark manipulators can resort to humor or sarcasm to make you feel inferior and insecure. They are trying to establish superiority over you by constantly marginalizing and ridiculing you. Don't let them get to you and reassure yourself that you are full of potential.

Don't take on responsibilities willy-nilly. The manipulator can use the classic "playing dumb" tactic to make you take on their own workload. For example, if a coworker is pretending they don't understand what you expect of them, knowing full well the project deadline is looming. You should call out their bluff and not let them get away with no work.

Don't give them leverage over you. If the manipulator is giving you the "silent treatment", don't get agitated and hold your ground. They are attempting to make you second guess yourself and asset power over you.

Get a grip on your soft side. The manipulator will always seek to take advantage of you and appeal to your soft spot. They will attempt to exploit your emotional weaknesses and vulnerabilities and use them as ammunitions against you.

Patience is a virtue! If you can control your anxiety and excitement, you are always in a better position to make rational decisions.

Self awareness. Knowing and acknowledging your strengths and weakness will help you design your defenses accordingly. When the manipulator is trying to strike a nerve to get an extreme reaction out of you and then subsequently guilt you into making decisions that will only help them, use your mental strength to overcome the manipulation.

Develop healthy coping mechanisms. We all go through ups and downs in life but a lot of people look to alcohol and overeating to distress. Remember there are no answers at the bottom of that bottle and carb coma will eventually lead to diseases.

Be easy on yourself. You are your own best friend! There is always a dawn after the dusk. We all cannot be good at just everything we ever decide to do. Learn you lesson and give yourself a break. Practice meditation to silence your mind and find inner peace.

Avoid being overly dependent on others. It's totally acceptable to seek help but if you develop chronic dependencies on others to resolve your problems, you will begin to undermine yourself and lose the confidence you need to protect yourself from the dark manipulator.

Give yourself pep talk every now and then. You can restore your metal health and well-being by saying uplifting affirmations to yourself. Positivity is the foundation of good mental health.

Conclusion

Thanks for reading this book.

A great deal of our emotions is expressed through our arms and hands. The warm embrace of a touch indicates love while a sharp slap translates to anger. Much of our productivity depends on the accuracy of our arms and hands when completing tasks. The movements of the arms and hands are quite obvious as they are used as a complement to verbal expression. Let's consider a few subliminal signals we receive from analyzing the hands and arms.

As our arms expand, we typically appear larger than our normal demeanor. This could be used as a descriptive means to explain how massive a person or object is, or this could be a subtle sign of instigating aggression or dominance. It also indicates spatial awareness. A person could expand the arms to give the subtle signal that they prefer space. It could be likened to "marking their territory." On the contrary, when the arms expand but curve towards the person, this is reminiscent of a hug. This embrace indicates safety or protection. Many mother figures are seen welcoming their children in this manner.

Since we primarily use our hands and arms to gesture, they are extremely descriptive tools that express our emotions. When the arms are raised, this is a sign of frustration and overwhelming doubt. We can almost envision an overwhelmed person clenching their hands over their ears or on top of the head as a means of protection.

The crossing of the arms is a true indicator of how a person is feeling. As previously mentioned, when the arms are crossed, this typically means anxiety, shyness, fear, or disbelief. We can picture a frustrated mother or father crossing their arms towards their child when they do something naughty. However, when the arms are tightly crossed with the hands either balled into fists or nestled in the armpits, this signals combat. This occurs when an individual has been taunted. Their anger is essentially holding their arms inward as a protective means. The hidden fists could signal the person holding themselves back from doing something they would regret.

Individuals who have been exposed to violence or who feel vulnerable may have a strong dislike for people speaking to them with their hands in their faces. Even a slight gesture could signal a fight or flight response.

When the arms are thrusting forward, this is a scare tactic usually intended to create emphasis. We fight with our arms and hands, so the connection between the two is threatening.

When the arms are positioned behind the backs and out of sight of the person they are engaging with, this indicates hidden intent. The person may lack confidence, or they are attempting to hide their fear through fiddling with their hands behind their backs. This isn't necessarily a sign of a liar. Rather, the person may simply feel uncomfortable, or they are preventing themselves from saying something.

The elbows, when facing out, could be a silent cry for space. A person may want others to back away from them without having to actually verbally express their disposition. This can easily be observed through the actions of children. Toddlers, who cannot communicate verbally, will often extend their elbows in a sharp motion in order to indicate space. As adults, we do this subconsciously as a means of inner protection.

The hands are quite detailed in their means of communication. One move of the hand can indicate an invitation while another movement could ignite conflict. When the hands are crossed with the thumbs tucked under, this is a signal of peace. East Indian gurus can be seen holding their hands in this way to express giving, peaceful natures. They wish to extend this light to others through their physical movements. When the hands are placed in front of the belly button, with the fingers touching and open palms, this is a symbol of dignity. The person is trying to show their partner that they are confident, professional, and conscientious. The hands are also key indicators of direction. We use our fingers to point towards areas of interest. When the hands are placed delicately on the knees with the palms down, this could indicate submission, especially when leaning towards the opposite person. Women usually engage in this stance while attempting to show interest in a flirtatious manner. Hand gestures can also indicate movement. When the palm is facing a person, this translates to dismissal and disapproval. The person is using their hands to physically block the other person from their sight.

When the hands are touching parts of the face, this could translate to brainstorming, boredom, or even decision making. When the palms are essentially holding the face and cheeks upward, this is a clear indicator of a person attempting to wake themselves up from a boring situation. It shows disinterest in the most obvious of ways. However, when the index finger is pointing towards certain areas of the face, a person could be deep in thought. The positioning of the fingers as well as the firmness of their grasp is telling.

Excessive shaking that permeates throughout the palms and into the fingers occurs during high stress situations. A person may be so nervous, their hands begin to shake uncontrollably. This also is a sign of intense hunger. The hands and fingers begin to grow unsteady, thus displaying the body's lack of food. Slight trembles can also occur when a person is being caught in a lie or confronted for a mistake. They may be so angry that the shakes are their way of expressing that anger.

We use our hands to describe the size and stature of certain things. Much like the arms, they are used to accentuate the gravity of a story, describe the weightiness of a subject, and even demonstrate movement. They are our primary way of gesturing, and they can add great excitement to a story or a conversation. When working together with the arms, the hands can be a great indicator of a person's confidence. Touching creates a sense of warmth and community that connects people together. When analyzed carefully, the movement of the hands and arms can tell us key clues about a person's disposition.

CPSIA information can be obtained
at www.ICGtesting.com
Printed in the USA
LVHW020302230221
679613LV00007B/367

9 781914 184491